The Warm and Wonderful Church Nursery

by

Lori Haynes Niles

and

Kim Sikes

Group
Loveland, Colorado

Dedication

To my nursery teacher, Carolyn Braswell, wherever you are. I believe the principles in this book are true because my life bears witness to the significance of early church experience. You made a difference. And to Aimee, Zach, Erin Elizabeth, and Matthew— the four little people who taught me everything I know about enjoying babies. You'll always be my favorite playmates of all!
Lori Haynes Niles

To the Lord, who continually blesses my life. God gave me two babies and a ministry where I could serve God's youngest creations.
Kim Sikes

The Warm and Wonderful Church Nursery

Visit our Web site: **www.grouppublishing.com**

Credits
Authors: Lori Haynes Niles and Kim Sikes
Editor: Jolene L. Roehlkepartain
Creative Development Editor: Jim Kochenburger
Chief Creative Officer: Joani Schultz
Copy Editor: Bob Kretschman
Art Director: Kari K. Monson
Cover Art Director: Jeff A. Storm
Computer Graphic Artist: Anita M. Cook
Cover Designer: Andrea Boven
Cover Photographers: Dynamic Graphics and Tony Stone
Illustrators: Benrei Huang and Dana C. Regan
Production Manager: Peggy Naylor

Unless otherwise noted, Scripture taken from the HOLY BIBLE, NEW INTERNATIONAL VERSION®. Copyright © 1973, 1978, 1984 by International Bible Society. Used by permission of Zondervan Publishing House. All rights reserved.

Library of Congress Cataloging-in-Publication Data
Niles, Lori Haynes, 1961–
      The warm and wonderful church nursery / by Lori Haynes Niles and Kim Sikes.
          p.   cm.
      Includes index.
      ISBN 0-7644-2090-9 (alk. paper)
      1. Christian education of preschool children. I. Sikes, Kim,
   1949-   . II. Title
   BV1539.N54 1999
   268'.432--dc21   99-28247
                                                                                                              CIP

10 9 8 7 6 5 4 3   08 07 06 05 04 03 02 01

Printed in the United States of America.

Contents

Introduction 5

Chapter 1: Together Time .9

Look-and-Laugh Books 10
Tunnel Tube 12
Baby Bubblers 14
Indoor Track 16
Pop-Up Puppet 18
Lift-and-Peek Books 20
Riding Roller 22
Soft-Touch Gloves 24

Chapter 2: Practical Playthings 27

Jingle Bands 28
Tumble Toys 30
Baby-Sized Soft Dolls 32
Baby Basketball 34
Wiggle Worm 36
Wave Maker 38
Cookie-Cutter Puzzles 40
Sandpaper Blocks 42
Water-Ballet Bags 44

Chapter 3: Appealing Art .47

Fancy, Fruity Finger Paint .48
Sticky Collages 50
Neat-Scoop Loops 52
Squeeze Art 54
Play Clay 56
Jelly Bags 58

Chapter 4: Cozy Corners 61

Wonderful, Whimsical Window Art .62
Parents' Peekaboo, One-Way Mirror 65
A Little Door of My Own 67
My Own Door With Wall Mural 69
Resting Rug 73
Reading Rug 75
Puzzle Rug 77
Road Rug 79
Activity-Wall Train 81
Learn-About-Me, Fun Flannel Board 82
Baby-Safe Bulletin Board 83
Mirror, Mirror, Who's That? 84
Magical Magnet Board 85
Baby Chalkboard 86

Chapter 5: Angel Aids 87

Shoulder Apron 88
Baby Directory 90
Pocket Belt 92
Boo-Boo Bags 94
Angel Quick Fixes 96

Appendixes

Appendix A: Nursery Manual Cover Page 97
Appendix B: A Nursery Mission Statement 98
Appendix C: Play Ideas for Toys .100
Appendix D: High-Tech Helpers .101
Appendix E: Establishing Peaceful Traditions 102
Appendix F: Songs for the Nursery 104
Appendix G: Funky Finger Puppets 107
Appendix H: Ten Ways to Use a Blanket 108
Appendix I: Ten Ways to Use a Blow-up Ball 109

Index 110

Introduction

A t a leadership conference of professional children's pastors, we learned the two dirtiest words in children's ministry: child care. Each time these words came up, there were snickers, snorts, and sighs. It wasn't because children's workers don't care for children or because they don't realize the value of quality child care for children of working parents. It was because those two words are so often used in the church to mean "just provide a place for babies to stay while the *real ministry* takes place in another room."

Your church's nursery ministry *is* real ministry. It's multifaceted. It's multidimensional. It's a multitargeted ministry. Your church nursery provides a mission field for those who are called to serve, a first impression for many new families, respite and training for parents, and most importantly, a child's first contact with the family of God outside his or her own home. It's a place where babies can learn that the God who created them is Lord of all there is to know. And it's a place where we become even more awed by the wonder of God through these newborn creations called babies.

The Ministry of the Nursery

God has blessed us with the opportunity to witness his bountiful blessings as we have ministered to babies and their families. We have had the privilege of ministering to many single parents who have brought their babies. One parent in particular was so stressed out from the responsibility of caring for her child that she looked forward to the respite of an hour or two. She found it in our church. When she first started bringing her son, she was frustrated that the baby screamed and clung to her. She clearly was annoyed by the scene and unsympathetic to her son. When the baby adjusted after a month or two, arrival time had changed to a happy event.

This was when we had the opportunity to really minister to the parent, helping her to fall even more in love with her baby—to see her baby with the same delight God finds in each one of us. We did this by giving this mother a full account of her baby's time with us, sharing all the cute and remarkable things he could do, and showing her activities she could do with him at home.

For this child, church and God became a real comfort. Although he has been out of the nursery for four years now, he still insists that his mother bring him to church. This child continues to lead his mother to God.

About This Book

This book was designed to give you tools to enrich each moment you spend in nursery ministry, to help you with ways to teach babies and parents the joy of belonging to God's family. You'll find lots of pick-and-choose options to tailor to your own specific set of needs. Each option will give you a simple tool to make for your nursery—a toy or teaching aid to construct from easy-to-find, low-cost materials—that will help you grab and hold a little one's attention.

The photocopiable page following the construction directions gives you ideas for how to use the tool effectively with babies of different ages. You'll find ideas for holders (babies age three to seven months old), crawlers (babies age seven to twelve months old), walkers (babies age twelve to twenty-four months old). Photocopy these pages as you create new tools and toys. Use the "Other Notes" portion of these pages to keep records of when the tool was used, which babies responded especially well to the activity, or other information that might prove helpful to another worker.

Perforate the pages with a three-hole punch, and put them in a binder to create a personalized nursery manual unique to your church. The manual will enable new and experienced volunteers to select activities to match the tools available in your nursery. Also include in your nursery manual information about your policies, traditions, and each enrolled baby. Use "Appendix A: Nursery Manual Cover Page" to create a cover for the manual. (You can slip a photocopy of the page into a three-ring notebook with a slide-on cover.) Then create tabbed divider pages for quick and easy reference.

Because the reproducible pages have practical ideas, you also can photocopy them to send home with parents. These pages can give parents ideas on how to interact with their babies at home. Use the "Other Notes" area to write a description of the nursery tool or to suggest home items parents can use to do the activity.

Not every activity has an obvious spiritual purpose. That's because, for babies, there are no real lines between what is secular and what is sacred. Yet God is the creator of every good and perfect gift (James 1:16-17). Reflect God's presence in your conversations with babies. Pray little prayers of gratitude as you talk with babies, saying "Thank you, God, for my little friend, C.J." or "We praise you, Lord, for things that spin!" Ask questions that focus babies on God, such as "Who made the elephant?" or "Do you think God knew bubbles would make you so happy?" Never miss an opportunity to teach the principles of Theology 101, which include "God loves you," "God gives us good things to enjoy," and "God is happy when you learn new things."

If you're looking for guidelines on how to set up a new nursery ministry or fortify an established one, see the book The Safe and Caring Church Nursery, *by Jennifer Root Wilger (Group Publishing, 1998). It's chock full of the basics to help you make sure you've thought through every detail of nursery planning.*

To use the tools in this book most effectively, follow these suggestions:

1. Get together with volunteers to have a construction party. Invite members of the congregation who enjoy making crafts. Make several items listed in this book at the same time for multiple babies. Follow up by trying to add at least one new item to your nursery collection each month.

2. Rotate your selections. Put some items in storage while keeping others on the floor during nursery hours. Remove the pages of your manual that correspond to items that are in storage, and then replace them when you return those items for use. This will keep your manual up to date.

3. Give regular volunteers each a copy of the nursery manual so they can have a copy at home to prepare for nursery times. This is even more helpful if you are using a nursery curriculum. Volunteers can think through which teaching tools will help them

maximize the learning goals for each lesson.

4. Spotlight an activity from time to time, demonstrating for parents what you and their babies are doing together.

5. Host a semiannual open house or family tea to keep parents posted about how you are meeting their babies' changing needs as they grow.

Your Call to Nursery Ministry

We pray that as you use these tools, God will reveal new ways to communicate his love to the children and families you work with. Make your nursery a haven, a sanctuary full of loving fun for the babies who spend time there. Let your caring relationship with each little person guide your interaction both inside and outside the nursery walls.

You will find, as we have, that for some families under stress, the best part of the babies' week is their time spent in the church nursery. It is the place where they meet God. It is the place where they feel God's comfort and safety through the ministry of a loving nursery staff. As you teach these tiny disciples, remember that you are helping to establish perceptions of God's house and people that will last a lifetime.

God has richly entrusted you and called you to true *ministry*.

Richest blessings on you and the babies you serve!

Lori Haynes Niles
Kim Sikes

Chapter 1

TOGETHER TIME

All time in the nursery is together time! The activities in this chapter involve items that should be used only by babies under the direct supervision of an adult. When playtime is over, put away the items in this chapter for another time.

For babies, play is work and work is play. As you play together, rejoice in the good God who gave you and the baby to each other. God has graced you with an ever-renewable supply of little brothers and sisters in Christ. Each time a baby is born, you have the privilege of investing in that child's spiritual growth. Help babies learn that talking to God is as natural as eating and sleeping. Talk about God as babies sit down and stand up, as they drift off to sleep and wake up, as they play and as they relax.

Here are activities to get you started.

Look-and-Laugh Books

Activity: *Babies will look and laugh at these cute and durable books about themselves and their friends.*

Purpose: *To help babies develop book-readiness skills that will lead them into a lifelong love of God's written word.*

Make-It Level: Medium preparation

Use-It Level: Low preparation

Materials Needed: Resealable freezer bags; photos of children in your class, familiar objects, or magazine pictures; assorted paper for mounting photos; scissors; glue stick; marker; tape; needle or sewing machine; heavy thread or yarn; decorative stickers (optional); and poster board (optional).

Getting Ready

Select twelve sheets of coordinating paper. Use either solid colors or printed paper located in the scrapbook section of your favorite craft store. Cut each piece one-quarter inch smaller than the dimensions of the resealable bag.

Trim around the photos so that only the person or object is left. Apply glue to the back of the photo cutout, and mount it on one of the sheets of paper. Decorative stickers may be added around the picture. Repeat the process on the second sheet of paper. Position the two sheets back to back, and slide them into a resealable bag.

Make a cover with a title to slide inside one of the bags. Stack the plastic "pages" in order, and temporarily hold them together with tape. Stitch the bags together along the bottom of the resealing line.

For an extra-sturdy book, mount the photos on poster board.

More Merriment

You may want to create a learning look-and-laugh book for older babies. For example, we found some scrapbook paper with a bee theme and created a book that shows our babies "bee-ing" kind, helpful, cheerful, loving, and happy.

Look-and-Laugh Books

How to Use This Item

With Holders (three to seven months old):

Have a baby sit on your lap. As you turn the pages, sing "Jesus Loves the Little Children."

With Crawlers (seven to twelve months old):

Set the baby on your lap or on the floor. Let the baby turn the pages. Identify the people in the picture and say: **Jesus loves** [child's name]. **Jesus loves** [another child's name]. At the end of the book, say: **And Jesus loves you!** Give the baby a big hug.

With Walkers (twelve to twenty-four months old):

Have the baby leaf through the pages to find pictures of specific people or items as you name them. For example, to Jennifer you might say, "Find the picture of Micah. Who loves Micah? Jesus loves Micah. I love Micah. Jennifer loves Micah. Where is Micah playing today?" Help the walker make a connection between the picture of Micah in the book and Micah in the nursery. Developing these kinds of mental connections between the book and real life can contribute to the ability to make a connection from God's Word to life application as children mature.

Maintenance Message

These books can be sanitized by wiping the pages with a 1:10 solution of isopropyl alcohol to water. Do not immerse the books.

Other Notes

Tunnel Tube

Activity: *Babies will play inside or crawl through a multipurpose tunnel.*

Purpose: *Use this versatile tool to provide a quiet space for younger babies and to encourage older babies' motor skills, or as a prop for storytelling.*

Make-It Level: Medium preparation

Use-It Level: Low preparation

Materials Needed: A new, large, plastic outdoor garbage can; a drill; a saber saw or reciprocating saw; sandpaper; a terry towel or blanket; and glow-in-the-dark paint (optional).

Getting Ready

Use the drill to make a hole in the bottom of the garbage can. Use the saw to cut a circle out of the plastic, leaving about two inches of the bottom still attached all the way around. Make sure not to cut off the entire bottom or the end of the tunnel will collapse. Sand around the edges to smooth away roughness.

If desired, paint stars or abstract designs on the inside with glow-in-the-dark paint. If you do this, activate the glow by putting a flashlight inside the tunnel for several minutes in preparation for each baby. Darken the tunnel by throwing a blanket over one end as you block the light from the other end with your body. Talk to the baby about the wonderful lights God placed in the dark sky. Use the "Other Notes" area of your notebook to cue your staff on this use for the tunnel.

More Merriment

Make this tunnel serve double duty as a stuffed animal storage bin during the week. At the end of your class time, turn the tunnel on its end, and let babies drop the stuffies into the tunnel to give the animals their turn.

Tunnel Tube

How to Use This Item

With Holders (three to seven months old):

• Lay a baby inside the tunnel lengthwise on his or her back, and gently rock the tunnel from side to side.

• Place a blanket in the tunnel first, and then slide the baby in through the narrow end of the tunnel on his or her tummy. Have someone on the other side pull the edges of the blanket and slide the baby along until he or she is completely out of the tunnel. If you don't have a teaching partner, place the baby in the tunnel and continue talking to him or her as you walk to the other side to pull the blanket. Make eye contact with the baby before you begin to pull.

With Crawlers (seven to twelve months old):

• Place the baby inside the tunnel horizontally, on his or her tummy. Slowly and gently begin to roll the tunnel so the child crawls around the inside of the tunnel. Keep one hand on the tunnel at all times to make sure the baby doesn't get the tunnel rolling too fast.

• Encourage the child to enter the tunnel on his or her own and crawl all the way through to you. Offer plenty of cheering for a job well done.

With Walkers (twelve to twenty-four months old):

• Turn the tunnel on its end. Put the child inside the tunnel, and encourage him or her to crouch down. Knock on the side of the tunnel, and say: **Is someone who loves Jesus in there?** Look over the edge to see the baby. Say: **There you are!** [Child's name] **loves Jesus!** As babies become familiar with the tunnel and get steady on their feet, cover the open end with a pillow, and let the baby pop the pillow off whenever he or she is ready.

• Place a flying disk upside down on the floor. Place the tunnel horizontally on top of it. Let one or more children get inside. Slowly spin the tunnel around on the disk as you say this chant:

Whirling, whirling round and round,
Jesus keeps me safe and sound.

Stop the spinning abruptly as you say the word "sound."

Other Notes

Storyteller Tales

Briefly tell one of the storm-at-sea stories from the Bible (such as Jesus walking on the water or the story of Jonah) as a baby lies inside the tunnel. Build the storm's intensity by tapping your fingernails lightly on the outside of the tunnel, then fingertips, then open hands. Watch for the baby's response to make sure he or she is not becoming frightened. The first signal he or she may give you is a widening of the eyes, followed by a scowl, or body tensing. Be sure to make all your Bible interactions with babies pleasant ones, as you represent the Living Word to these little ones.

Baby Bubblers

Activity: *Babies will watch the dance of hundreds of tiny bubbles and hear about God the creator.*

Purpose: *To stimulate visual tracking and hand-eye coordination as you reinforce that God made all things.*

Make-It Level: Medium preparation

Use-It Level: Medium preparation

Materials Needed: For each Bubbler, you'll need seven plastic straws, a rubber band, and masking tape. For the solution, you'll need a watertight plastic container, $1/3$ cup clear liquid dishwashing soap, $1/2$ gallon of water, and six teaspoons of glycerin (available from a pharmacy). For a version good for just one day, try substituting white corn syrup for the glycerin.

Getting Ready

Gather the seven straws in your hand. This should form a ring of straws with one in the center, leaving little space between the straws. Fasten them together with a rubber band, and tape around the rubber band for extra security.

Mix the ingredients in the bubble solution with a light touch. If the mixture becomes too frothy, allow it to sit for several hours before using.

More Merriment

• Use commercial bubble solution for a quicker preparation time. Create bigger bubbles by experimenting with kitchen tools; berry baskets; plastic containers, such as film canisters, with both ends removed; or even clothes hangers. Whatever the shape of the blower, bubbles will always end up perfectly round if they don't pop in the process. It's an unalterable scientific principle set in place by the design of our great Creator and easily observed by the youngest scientists in your nursery.

• Attach one of the following rhyme activities to the bubble solution container to use when you blow bubbles:

Bubbles, bubbles, round, round, round. *God made you to float without a sound.* (Say: **Shhhh! Listen to the bubble!**)	**The Bubble Song** (to the tune of "Alouette") *Bubbles, bubbles, tiny little bubbles,* *Bubbles, bubbles, when are you going to pop?* (Help the baby touch and pop a bubble.)

Baby Bubblers

How to Use This Item

With Holders (three to seven months old):

Open the bubble solution, and place it out of the babies' reach. Hold a baby in your arms. Use one hand to dip the Bubbler into the solution. Blow into the Bubbler without touching your lips to the straws. The Bubbler will release scores of tiny bubbles with each gentle puff. Encourage the baby to watch the bubbles float and to reach out for them. It's fun to move the baby around within the bubble shower, but guard against the baby looking up and getting bubbles in his or her eyes.

With Crawlers (seven to twelve months old):

Let the baby sit on your lap or on the floor. Use one hand to dip the Bubbler into the solution. From behind the baby, blow into the Bubbler without touching your lips to the straws. The Bubbler will release scores of tiny bubbles in front of the baby with each gentle puff. Help the baby determine the source of the bubbles. Ask: **Where are all those bubbles coming from? Are you taking a bath up there?** Pretend to scrub the baby from head to toe. Show the baby how to fan the bubbles with his or her hands, or encourage blowing. Note that as bubbles fall on the floor, they pop. If they don't pop, clap the bubbles against the floor. Say: **Bye-bye bubbles!** as they pop. Say: **Thank you, God, for tiny bubbles and so much fun.**

With Walkers (twelve to twenty-four months old):

In addition to the activities described for younger children, walkers will enjoy chasing the bubbles. Show them how to clap the bubbles between their hands. As they chase them, say this chant:

God made bubbles to float so high.
God made me to catch them as they fly.

Dribble some solution on a tabletop, and then dip the Bubbler in the solution, hold it about a half-inch from the table, and blow mounds of bubbles for walkers to explore. Make sure walkers' hands are washed before they touch their faces.

Maintenance Message

It's best to do this activity on a sheet tossed over the carpet or bare floor (wiping frequently to keep the floor from becoming slippery). Bubble residue can cause carpet to hold dirt.

Other Notes

Indoor Track

Activity: Babies will use this open-ended setup in a variety of ways.

Purpose: To provide practice in developing balance skills and real-life experience with boundaries and obstacles.

Make-It Level: Low preparation

Use-It Level: Low preparation

Materials Needed: Masking tape and other readily available classroom supplies, such as string, blankets, blocks, or toys (depending on the activity).

Getting Ready

Lay a strip of masking tape across your floor space. Place a parallel strip of tape about eighteen inches away from the first strip to form a path. The path may be straight, or it may be made into a zigzag pattern by using a series of shorter parallel strips. To make the path more challenging for older babies, make it an even more winding path or a path that widens and narrows.

More Merriment

Pull a segment of tape about fourteen inches long, and then attach twelve twelve-inch-long strips to it so that it looks like a ladder. Lay this down on the floor, sticky sides of the attached pieces up. Tape around all the edges to hold it securely to the floor. Watch how children respond as they walk or crawl over this sticky square. It makes a fun sound and provides an interesting kinesthetic experience as well.

Indoor Track

How to Use This Item

With Holders (three to seven months old):

Lay a baby down on back or tummy on a blanket at the beginning of the tape track. Pull the edges of the blanket to navigate him or her along the trail. As you pull, chant:

> *Clickity-clack, Clickity-clack,*
> *I'm chugging along this railroad track.*
> *Clickity-clack, Clickity-clack,*
> *I'm following Jesus, won't turn back!*

Turn the baby around, and head back the other direction.

With Crawlers (seven to twelve months old):

• Attach a string to a toy, and pull it along the track as you encourage a baby to follow the toy. Cheer the baby on with words such as "Stay on the track," or "Don't touch the lines."

• Hold the child's hands, and bounce the child along inside the lines as you follow the actions of this chant:

> *Walking, walking, hop, hop, hop,*
> *Between the lines, and now we stop.*

Say: **Thank you God for straight paths. Help** [child's name] **to walk in your paths all her life!**

With Walkers (twelve to twenty-four months old):

• Add some obstacles to the path. Make "crossbars" with tape to form a ladder on the floor, and encourage the child to take one step in each square. Or put a row of blocks in the path and encourage the child to step over it. Offer to hold the hand of any child who hesitates.

• Show the child how to push a car or other rolling toy along the path. Encourage him or her to not touch the lines, and offer praise for each effort. Talk about pushing slowly, not getting in a hurry, and being careful. These are skills we all have to apply to lifelong spiritual growth.

Maintenance Message

Remove masking tape at the end of each class session to keep the adhesive from transferring from the tape to the carpet.

Other Notes

Pop-Up Puppet

Activity: *Babies will get surprise affirmation from a peekaboo puppet.*

Purpose: *To help establish a fun and loving atmosphere in the nursery, or to distract a fussy baby.*

Make-It Level: High preparation

Use-It Level: Low preparation

Materials Needed: A twelve- to sixteen-ounce plastic tumbler; ½ yard of fabric that matches the color of the tumbler; measuring tape; a drill; scissors; needle and thread (optional); a wooden spoon with a handle approximately two times the height of the tumbler; two pieces of one-eighth-inch ribbon that matches the fabric, with one piece about ½ yard long and the other piece about ¾ yard; tacky glue; a candle; black permanent marker; and other optional items to decorate the spoon as a face, such as synthetic hair, a small hat, a tiny pompom for the nose, and wiggly eyes.

Getting Ready

Draw a cute face on the wooden spoon with a permanent marker (see the model on page 19 for ideas). If you'd like, glue on synthetic hair, a small hat, a tiny pompom nose, or wiggly eyes since the baby won't use this puppet directly.

Next, measure the height of the tumbler. Cut a circle of fabric whose diameter is two times the height of the tumbler. Fold the circle in quarters, and snip about one-eighth of an inch from the corner fold to make a small hole in the center of the circle. Apply tacky glue just below the bowl of the wooden spoon, and then slip the spoon handle through the small hole in the circle of fabric. Use the half-yard of ribbon to tie the fabric around the spoon handle at the glue line. You now have a spoon puppet with a long flowing robe. At this point, you may choose to use the needle and thread to make a long basting stitch around the bottom edge of the puppet's robe. Pull the thread to gather the bottom of the robe evenly to the approximate diameter of the plastic tumbler's rim.

In the bottom of the plastic tumbler, drill a hole large enough to accommodate the spoon handle. Push the spoon handle through the inside bottom of the cup. Apply a layer of tacky glue all around the outer rim of the tumbler. Attach the bottom of the robe to the outer rim of the tumbler. Tightly tie the three-quarter-yard ribbon around the rim to secure the fabric. Pull the handle of the spoon down to draw the puppet inside the tumbler. Rub a candle along the handle to help it slide through the hole more easily.

More Merriment

Experiment with the range of motion your little pop-up friend has. Move the handle from side to side and around in circles to make the puppet dance.

Pop-Up Puppet

How to Use This Item

With Babies of All Ages:

• Name your puppet. Call the puppet by name.

• Use the puppet as a greeter. Before the baby leaves Mom or Dad's arms, let the baby tap on the outside of the cup. Older babies can call the puppet's name. Tell the baby how glad the puppet is that he or she is here...and how glad you are, too.

• Let the puppet say goodbye to each baby with this action song to the tune of "(Here We Go) Looby Loo":

Give baby a goodbye kiss (Pop up the puppet, and touch it to the baby's cheek.)

Give baby a goodbye kiss,

Give baby a goodbye kiss,

And wave bye-bye, like this. (Use your other hand to wave goodbye, and encourage the baby to wave back.)

• Anytime, sing "If You're Happy and You Know It." Use the words, "If Jesus loves you and you know it, pop right up!" Play around with the puppet's response time to get a laugh from each baby.

• Try using the puppet to play peekaboo with a fussy baby.

• Have the puppet move in time to praise music.

Maintenance Message

If the glue on the puppet loosens, wrap some duct tape around the fabric and the cup.

Other Notes

Lift-and-Peek Books

Activity: *Babies will peek behind doors to find picture answers to story questions.*

Purpose: *To encourage early critical thinking skills, preparing children to later participate in reading God's Word.*

Make-It Level: Medium preparation

Use-It Level: Low preparation

Materials Needed: For each lift-and-peek book, you'll need a spiral-bound book of index cards or watercolor paper, a cutting blade, stickers, colored tape, a pen or marker, and a glue stick.

Getting Ready

Select a theme for your lift-and-peek book, and purchase stickers to go with it. Here are some suggestions to get you started:

• Who did God make to say...? (an animal theme)

• What does the baby do when...? (a theme about the baby's routine. The last question could be "And who loves the baby most of all?" Accompany the question with a sticker picture of Jesus.)

• What kind of a home did God create for...? (an environment theme)

Write the first question on the first page of the spiral book. Cut three sides of a square slightly larger than the sticker to make a door in this page. This door may open in any direction. Raise the door, and attach a two-and-one-half inch strip of tape to the side of the door opposite the "hinge," forming a handle that extends beyond the edge of the door (see illustration on p. 21). Apply glue to the back of the first page, leaving the door open. Press the first page firmly against the second page. Then put the sticker that answers the question on the second page so that it will be covered by the door. These two pages form the first page of the book.

More Merriment

Watercolor paper is thick enough that you can paste thin, textured objects under the doors. Try "What's soft as a bunny's fur?" with a piece of velvet glued under the door, or "What's rough as a fish scale?" with sandpaper underneath.

Lift-and-Peek Books

How to Use This Item

With Holders (three to seven months old):

Sit with a child in your lap. Read the questions of the lift-and-peek book to the baby in a singsong voice. Open the doors for him or her.

With Crawlers (seven to twelve months old):

Sit with the child in your lap. Read the questions of the lift-and-peek book in a singsong voice. Encourage the baby to lift the answer doors. After looking at each answer, thank God for the object named.

With Walkers (twelve to twenty-four months old):

Hold a child in your lap. In addition to a traditional reading, let the child lift the doors first, and then let him or her help you say the question. (This works especially well with the animal book, "Who did God make to say...?" Babies can help you make the animal sounds.) These books are designed to encourage the child to verbalize and participate in the reading experience. Be sure to thank God for God's creation and provision as you read together.

Maintenance Message

Because these books are somewhat fragile, store them out of babies' reach, using them only for together time.

Other Notes

Riding Roller

Activity: *Babies will do a series of activities with the help of the riding roller.*

Purpose: *To develop balance as infants experience movements of praise.*

Make-It Level: Medium preparation

Use-It Level: Low preparation

Materials Needed: For each roller, you'll need a segment of a carpet roll twenty-four to thirty-six inches long (check with carpet retailers to obtain this; many times, they'll even saw the roll into segments for you); a segment of one-inch-thick foam that is twenty-four to thirty-six inches long (check with your foam supplier to see if he or she will bond it for you if you bring in the carpet roll); spray adhesive (check to make sure foam is one of the items the brand is effective for); one and one-half yards of forty-five-inch fabric; and two rubber bands.

Getting Ready

Apply spray adhesive over the exterior of the carpet roll. Cover the roll with foam. Use the spray adhesive to bond the edges of the foam. When the adhesive is dry, roll the entire piece in the fabric, starting at one finished side and rolling it all the way to the other. Gather the leftover fabric at each end and secure it with rubber bands close to the carpet roll. Push it inside the hollow space, if desired.

More Merriment

For a different textural experience for the baby, use a terry bath towel or a plastic tablecloth to cover the roller. Also experiment with foam of different thickness.

Riding Roller

How to Use This Item

With Holders (three to seven months old):

• Place a baby on his or her tummy across the roller with arms extending over it, knees on the floor. Hold the baby by the waist. Rock the roller back and forth in time to some upbeat praise music.

• Place a toy on the floor in front of the roller. Place the baby on his or her tummy across the roller. Holding the baby at the waist, very slowly roll the baby forward toward the toy. Encourage him or her to stretch and reach for the toy. As the baby becomes more familiar with this motion, move your hands lower on his or her body until the baby is comfortable with you holding his or her ankles.

With Crawlers (seven to twelve months old):

• Lay the baby on his or her tummy, full body along the roller. Hold on to him or her at the thighs or waist. Rock the roller from side to side, continuing to support him or her as you rock, creating a bit more sophisticated balance challenge for older babies. Sing or play praise music to give you a rhythm for your rock.

With Walkers (twelve to twenty-four months old):

• Have a child stand in front of the roller as you kneel beside him or her. Ask the child to choose a doll to place on the roller. Roll the doll together as you say:

God can move a mountain or roll a mighty sea,
The great big God who does all this
Walks along with me!
God can move a mountain or roll a mighty sea.
The great big God who does all this
Loves little me!

• Help the child straddle the roller as you hold him or her under the arms. Show him or her how to push off with one foot and land on the other in time to upbeat praise music. At first, you will have to gently push the baby from side to side, but soon you'll be there only to provide minimal support as his or her legs take over.

Maintenance Message

Remove the outer cover, and launder it with the crib sheets.

Other Notes

Soft-Touch Gloves

Activity: *Brush babies' skin with different textures.*

Purpose: *To help babies appreciate the different textures God gave for their pleasure.*

Make-It Level: Low preparation

Use-It Level: Low preparation

Materials Needed: A glove; fabric glue; scissors; and scraps of four of the following materials: velvet, satin, synthetic fur, vinyl, or grosgrain ribbon.

Getting Ready

Put on the glove. Measure and cut a finger-length piece of each of the materials you selected. Put glue on each of the fingers of the glove while it is still on your hand. Apply a different material to each of the four fingers. Do not apply anything to the thumb. Let the glue set lightly before removing the glove.

More Merriment

Make sound gloves instead of soft-touch gloves. Glue a bottle cap to the tip of the thumb, a button to the first finger, sandpaper to the middle finger, and some corrugated cardboard or paper to the ring finger. Sew a jingle bell to the pinky. Explore the sounds each item makes against the bottle cap. Make sure that babies do not touch these gloves because the small items might pose a choking hazard. If you create this option, make a note of it on your reproducible manual page.

Soft-Touch Gloves

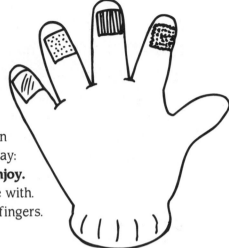

How to Use This Item

With Babies of All Ages:

• Hold the baby on your lap, putting your hand out in front of the baby. Encourage him or her to stroke one gloved finger at a time with his or her whole hand or index finger.

• Lightly rub one gloved finger at a time up and down the baby's arm, cheek, or tummy. Don't forget the thumb! Say: **Ooh! Soft satin! I'm so glad God gave us soft things to enjoy.**

• Let babies point to the finger they want you to stroke with.

• Tap your way up the baby's arm with two different fingers.

Maintenance Message

Hand-wash and air-dry the gloves.

Other Notes

Chapter 2
PRACTICAL PLAYTHINGS

Holders explore their world with their eyes and gradually expand their exploration by reaching out and grasping. Crawlers move toward interesting items and often find other stimulating diversions along the way. Walkers use not only their legs to explore but also their fingers, hands, and arms, which experiment with more advanced movements every day.

That's why it's important to have a nursery full of practical playthings. Babies need objects to explore and learn from at their own pace. The playthings in this chapter can be used in two ways: Introduce them to babies, or make them available so babies can explore them on their own during downtime.

Remember that it is part of God's plan for these little ones to grow in wisdom, in stature, and in favor with God. As you provide a rich environment for babies, you are giving them wonderful opportunities to become all that God would have them to be.

Here are some practical playthings to get you started.

Jingle Bands

Activity: Babies will be rewarded with a jingling sound each time they move their hands or feet.

Purpose: To help babies become aware of their ability to cause a reaction, and to develop an early love of praise through music.

Make-It Level: Medium preparation

Use-It Level: Low preparation

Materials Needed: Brightly colored stretch headbands (available in the hair accessories department), half-inch jingle bells, needle, and thread.

Getting Ready

For each band, lay the headband flat on a table. Pull apart the two halves of the doubled band, and whipstitch three jingle bells to the inside of the fabric. Whipstitch all around the headband to encase the bells. Pull the ends together to form a one and one-half-inch diameter ring. Whipstitch the ends together.

More Merriment

Use a high-contrast color yarn to make three big cross-stitches on the outer band as you sew in the jingle bells. Priests who served in the Temple during Bible times wore bells attached to the hems of their robes. Bells have been associated with serving God for thousands of years!

Jingle Bands

How to Use This Toy

With Holders (three to seven months old):

Place the jingle bands on the baby's wrist or ankle. Gently shake his or her arm or leg to demonstrate the sound it makes, and then give the baby time to experiment with moving his or her arm or leg while sitting or lying in a protected area such as a baby seat. It's an important developmental task for babies to establish the concept of cause and effect as they play with toys that allow them to make something happen. In this case, when they move, they hear a sound.

With Crawlers (seven to twelve months old):

Let babies move along with these bands on their wrists or ankles, especially when you need to monitor the movements of a particular child while your attention is directed toward another baby (such as during a diaper change). That way you can focus on one child and be completely aware of the whereabouts of another. Begin to articulate the concept that God always knows exactly where we are, even when we think God's not looking.

With Walkers (twelve to twenty-four months old):

Encourage children to hold the jingle bands as soft musical instruments. Give them to several babies at once, and lead the "Bell Band" as you play praise music in the background.

Sing babies this little song to the tune of "Jingle Bells":

Praising bells, praising bells
Singing out their song!
How I love to shake my bells
And praise God all day long!

Put the bells on their ankles or around their feet, and let them lie on their backs and kick their feet in time to the music.

Maintenance Message

Toss jingle bands in the washer on gentle cycle, and dry them in the dryer.

Other Notes

Tumble Toys

Activity: *Babies will roll these tumblers to watch the varied and interesting effects and experience the physical sensations of floating, turning over, and rolling.*

Purpose: *To give babies a simple and inexpensive variety of rolling toys, and to provide a common point of interest for babies and adults to interact around.*

Make-It Level: Low preparation

Use-It Level: Low preparation

Materials Needed: Glue, electrical tape, and food coloring or watercolor paint (optional). Make a whole box of tumble toys by combining the following materials in unique ways:

• Choose one of the following containers—a sixteen- to twenty-ounce clear, cylindrical drink bottle, or a two-liter soda bottle (colored bottles give a completely different look to the contents), with lids.

• Choose one or a combination of the following fillers—shaped craft beads, Mylar confetti, glitter, pompoms, jingle bells, tiny plastic toys, marbles, sequins of all shapes, plastic gems, nuts, bolts, and washers.

• Choose one of the following liquids with varying viscosity—water, vegetable oil, baby oil, and white corn syrup. (Do not mix white corn syrup with water because this combination will react chemically as it sits).

Getting Ready

Place your selection of fillers in the bottom of the container. Start out with just a few objects, and maybe some glitter. Add liquid, filling the bottle to the top of the neck. If you wish, add food coloring or watercolor paint. Put the lid on, and turn the bottle over to watch what happens. If you like the effect, apply glue around the lid, and screw it on tightly. If you are not satisfied with the way it looks, add more items. When you're satisfied, glue the lid on, and secure it on the outside with electrical tape.

Some objects will float, some will sink, and some will remain suspended for long periods of time. Make different variations. You might leave an air space in the bottle and watch what happens. You might draw a face on a bead with a permanent marker or put in one wiggly eye to encourage observation skills when you ask a baby to find it. Make silent tumblers by placing pompoms in an empty bottle. Add soap to a bottle filled with colored water to create enclosed bubbles to watch. Color the corn syrup dark blue, and add gold confetti stars to create a model of the night sky. Use your creativity—the possibilities are endless!

More Merriment

Make a Magnet Mitt by gluing a disk magnet inside a child-size mitten, near the fingertips. Place the other mitten inside the Magnet Mitt, pushing the thumb of the inner mitten inside the thumb of the outer mitten. Stitch the mitten cuffs together around the edges, and tack the fingertips to completely encase the magnet. Place lightweight screws or washers in an empty plastic bottle. Glue on the lid and secure with tape. Put the Magnet Mitt on a baby's hand. Hold the bottle on its side, and show the baby how to move the objects around with it.

Tumble Toys

How to Use This Toy

With Holders (three to seven months old):

• Hold a baby in your lap, and turn a tumble toy upside down and right side up several times. Watch to see if the baby is attracted to the movement. A tumble toy with fast-moving objects is best for the youngest babies.

• Talk about floating. An alert and comfortable baby will enjoy the sensation of floating in mid-air when you hold him or her away from your body. Or lay the baby on the floor on a soft blanket on his or her tummy. Place one hand against the baby's upper back for support, and pull the edges of the blanket to make the baby roll over.

With Crawlers (seven to twelve months old):

• Let babies encounter these tumble toys on their own as they play.

• Talk about upside down and right side up as you turn over the bottle. Sit with a baby on your lap, and turn him or her over against your legs. Say: **Now *you're* upside down. Let's turn you right side up.** Repeat this if the baby is having fun.

• Babies who crawl also can have fun rolling. Lay several blankets end to end on the floor, and encourage the baby to roll several times in a row.

With Walkers (twelve to twenty-four months old):

• Insist that children sit down as they play with these toys on the floor.

• Encourage children to locate one specific thing in the tumble toy, such as a red bead or the big star.

• Let children experience upside down as they put their heads toward the floor. Walkers can roll over safely if their chins are pressed against their chests.

Maintenance Message

Check the security of the lids each time you use these toys because the objects inside each tumbler could pose a choking hazard. Wipe the outside of the bottle with a 1:3 solution of iso-propyl alcohol to water.

Other Notes

Baby-Sized Soft Dolls

Activity: *Babies will love interacting with these soft, life-sized dolls.*

Purpose: *To involve babies in learning skills that will transfer to how they care for people.*

Make-It Level: Medium preparation

Use-It Level: Low preparation

Materials Needed: For each doll, you'll need a newborn-sized, footed sleeper with a collar; a newborn-sized snow hat; a leg cut from a nylon stocking; a needle; thread; about sixteen ounces of fiberfill; and fabric glue. (Note: Ask parents to donate outgrown sleepers and hats so you can make a new doll for the price of a bag of fiberfill and fifteen minutes of time.)

Getting Ready

Attach the snow hat to the sleeper by using the needle and thread to tack the back of the hat to the neck of the sleeper. Set it aside.

Form a firm, head-sized ball of fiberfill. Push it down to the center of the nylon stocking leg. Tie the ends of the leg together, forming a knot under the ball. Then tie several knots on top of each other at each end of the leg to resemble a tight little fist on each side.

Push the nylon ball into the hat, and each of the ends through the armholes of the sleeper. Whipstitch the cuffs closed around the little nylon fists. Take a couple of stitches through the edge of each fist to hold it securely to the cuff of the sleeper. The arms will draw back toward the sleeper. Stuff the remainder of the fiberfill into the sleeper, pushing it down into the legs and arms. Snap all the closings of the sleeper. Arrange the head at the proper angle, and use the needle and thread to tack the head in place.

Use fabric glue to glue between the snaps so the sleeper will not come open. Run a line of fabric glue around the head and neck to hold them in place. After the glue dries, fluff the doll so it's puffy in all the right places.

More Merriment

• These dolls look fine without any facial features, but if you'd like, stitch on eyes, a nose, and a mouth. Brush on a little blusher to highlight rosy cheeks.

• Attach a loop of elastic to each doll foot, and loop the elastic around older walkers' feet or ankles to make a "Walk-With-Me" doll.

Baby-Sized Soft Dolls

How to Use This Toy

With Holders (three to seven months old):
• Use one or more of these dolls as pillows to prop up little ones in a swing or infant seat.
• Let the doll give each baby a wrap-around hug.

With Crawlers (seven to twelve months old):
• Encourage babies to identify the doll's body parts.
• Encourage gentleness that will extend toward younger babies as you sing this song to the tune of "Are You Sleeping":

Gently, gently,

Gently, gently,

Pat the hands, pat the feet.

Touch them very softly; touch them very gently,

Baby's sweet, baby's sweet.

With Walkers (twelve to twenty-four months old):
• Babies will drag these little playmates everywhere they go! Encourage them to rock the babies in their arms and treat them lovingly. Talk about how we care for little babies like God cares for us.
• Sing "He's Got the Whole World in His Hands," using the verse "He's got the tiny little baby…"

Maintenance Message
Wash the doll in the gentle cycle and tumble dry when it becomes dirty. Do this only after the fabric glue is fully cured.

Other Notes

Baby Basketball

Activity: *Babies will toss beanbags into a laundry basket.*

Purpose: *To develop hand-eye coordination and large-muscle skill.*

Make-It Level: Medium preparation

Use-It Level: Low preparation

Materials Needed: Old socks with no holes, dry beans, scissors, and a round laundry basket.

Getting Ready

Put about one-half cup of beans in the toe of a sock, and tie it tightly closed. Cut off the excess material. Place the sock into a second sock, and tie tightly. Make several different beanbags, varying the amount of beans you use, so you can talk about heavy and light as babies play.

Put all the beanbags in the laundry basket, and set the laundry basket in a corner of the nursery. The wall will act as a backboard when babies toss the beanbags, increasing the likelihood of the babies' success.

More Merriment

Cut holes in the side of a cardboard box. Cut off the top flaps. Set the box against a wall, open side down, and let the babies put the beanbags through the holes.

Baby Basketball

How to Use This Toy

With Holders (three to seven months old):

Give one of the beanbags to a baby, and stand over the laundry basket. Encourage the baby to drop it in while you hold the baby. Cheer when the baby does, reinforcing the concept that it makes you happy when he or she does what you ask. This concept will later extend to an understanding that God is pleased when we obey.

With Crawlers (seven to twelve months old):

Let babies sit near the basket. Encourage them to toss the beanbags in the basket. Clap and cheer at their successes. Sing this song of affirmation to the tune of "London Bridge," using the names of children from your nursery:

[Child's name]***'s growing big and strong, big and strong, big and strong!***
[Child's name]***'s growing big and strong, like God planned!***

With Walkers (twelve to twenty-four months old):

• Encourage babies to stand and toss beanbags into the basket. Move them back little by little to increase the challenge.

• Talk about the differences in the beanbags. Encourage babies to pick up the beanbag you specify, such as "Get the big beanbag," or "Find the striped beanbag." Watch their actions, and notice when they make discoveries such as it's easier to throw a lighter one from farther back. This requires the kind of complex cause-and-effect thinking that babies do without being able to talk about.

• Use the beanbags in balance activities, such as this action song to the tune of "If You're Happy and You Know It":

Put the beanbag on your head, on your head.
Put the beanbag on your head, on your head.
Put the beanbag on your head, then take some little steps,
With the beanbag on your head, on your head.

Substitute the word "head" with the words "shoulder" or "back" for older walkers.

Maintenance Message

Check the beanbags periodically to make sure the knots are tight and there are no holes to let the beans escape; the beans are a choking hazard. If there are any problems, remove the beans, and replace the sock.

Other Notes

Wiggle Worm

Activity: *Babies will take delight in discovering the surprises in this little, green worm.*

Purpose: *To stimulate tactile and auditory exploration.*

Make-It Level: High preparation

Use-It Level: Low preparation

Materials Needed: One leg of a pair of girls' green opaque tights; fiberfill; plastic grocery bags (enough to make a tennis ball-sized ball when wadded up); a half-inch diameter jingle bell; two 1½-inch by 1½-inch squares of fabric; fabric glue; four small terry ponytail holders (from the hair accessories department); twelve inches of the following types of ribbon: satin, velvet, and lace; twenty-four inches of grosgrain ribbon; scissors; and fabric paint.

Getting Ready

At least twenty-four hours before you are ready to construct the Wiggle Worm, cut the grosgrain ribbon in half. On one of the pieces, make random dots of fabric paint, and let it dry to create a bumpy textured ribbon. Put fabric glue around all four edges of one of the squares of fabric. Set the jingle bell on top, and then press the other square of fabric into the glue to encase the bell. Let it dry.

Stuff the leg of the opaque tights with fiberfill to the halfway point. Put the encased jingle bell in, and add another handful of fiberfill. Then put in the plastic grocery bags, loosely wadded into a tennis ball-sized ball. Add fiberfill to within two inches of the end of the tights. Tie the end closed. Cut off any excess.

Put the ponytail holders evenly spaced around the stuffed tube. Round the area between each ponytail holder by holding one end of the worm in each hand and compressing it.

Put a layer of fabric glue on the back of each ribbon. Wrap each of the five ribbons around a different segment of the wiggle worm. Lift each of the ponytail holders, and squeeze a line of glue under each one to hold them firmly in place. Let the worm dry thoroughly.

More Merriment

Embroider on black eyes, and add a tiny stitch of white thread to the eyes to give your worm character.

Wiggle Worm

How to Use This Toy

With Babies of All Ages:

• Allow the babies to freely explore the Wiggle Worm.

• Sing this song to the tune of "Camptown Races," varying the texture word as appropriate:

Little worm, I feel your back

Bumpy, bumpy (Change these words to "lacy," "silky," "velvety," or "scratchy" depending on which ribbon the baby is touching.)

Little worm, I feel your back

Bumpy all day long.

Thank God I can feel

All the things I feel,

Little worm I feel your back

Bumpy all day long.

• Extend babies' play by teaching them to wiggle their index fingers as you sing this song to the tune of "Johnny Works With One Hammer":

Little worms go wiggle, wiggle, wiggle.

Little worms go wiggle, just like you! (Tickle the baby's tummy for wiggly fun.)

Maintenance Message

Sanitize this critter by misting it with a 1:10 solution of isopropyl alcohol to water, but don't immerse it.

Other Notes

Wave Maker

Activity: *Babies will roll and tumble this wave maker as they learn about the God who made the mighty oceans.*

Purpose: *To encourage a controlled, side-to-side movement, which also promotes balance.*

Make-It Level: Low preparation

Use-It Level: Low preparation

Materials Needed: A twenty-ounce or two-liter plastic soda bottle, water, blue food coloring, glitter, vegetable oil, electrical tape, and white glue.

Getting Ready

Fill the soda bottle three quarters full with water. Add blue food coloring, and sprinkle in about a teaspoon of glitter. Pour in vegetable oil to within a quarter inch of the top. Put glue around the inside edges of the bottle cap before screwing it on. Secure the cap to the bottle with electrical tape.

When the bottle is rocked side to side, it resembles ocean waves.

More Merriment

Add little plastic sea creatures, seascape confetti, or tiny seashells and sand before sealing the bottle.

Wave Maker

How to Use This Toy

With Babies of All Ages:

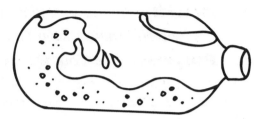

• Rock the Wave Maker from side to side in the baby's field of vision. Sing this song to the tune of "Matchmaker" from the musical *Fiddler on the Roof*:

> **Wave Maker, Wave Maker, make me a wave,**
> **Give it some splash, give it some spray.**
> **I am amazed at the work of God's hands,**
> **The ocean that God has made!**

• Support the bottle in the baby's hands, and encourage a steady, rhythmic side-to-side motion. Watching the waves can be a wonderfully soothing experience for a fussy baby.

• Play one of the many commercially produced recordings that feature ocean sounds or ocean sounds with music. These often can be borrowed from the public library.

• Talk about the sparkling water. Hold the bottle up to a natural light source to intensify the effect.

• Let babies roll the bottle across the floor on their own.

Maintenance Message

Wipe the bottle with a 1:10 solution of isopropyl alcohol to water.

Other Notes

Cookie-Cutter Puzzles

Activity: *Babies will match the shape of a cookie cutter to a hole and turn it so that it fits.*

Purpose: *To encourage problem-solving skills.*

Make-It Level: Medium preparation

Use-It Level: Medium preparation

Materials Needed: For each puzzle, you need a sheet of craft foam, one or more plastic cookie cutters in shapes of things that God made, a fine-tip marking pen, and scissors.

Getting Ready

For each puzzle, place the cookie cutters you will use on the foam, and carefully trace around the bottom edge of each one. Carefully cut around the interior of the line you drew for a snug fit when the cookie cutter is inserted. Save the shapes you cut from foam to do a reverse puzzle with the older babies, letting them match the shapes to the cookie cutters.

More Merriment

Your cookie cutters can serve double duty as tools for modeling dough.

Cookie-Cutter Puzzles

How to Use This Toy

With Holders (three to seven months old):

Start with one-piece puzzles. Even young babies can grasp and manipulate the cookie cutters, and the foam won't slip around as the baby tries to insert them. Start with one cookie cutter on a piece of foam, and move up in complexity. Let the baby hold the cookie cutter, and guide his or her hand to put the piece in the hole (which is the empty space cut from the foam). Offer lots of clapping if all the baby does is let go of the piece.

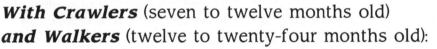

With Crawlers (seven to twelve months old)
and Walkers (twelve to twenty-four months old):

• Sit with the baby. Use a two-piece puzzle. Give him or her one cookie cutter at a time, and encourage him or her to find the hole. As the baby becomes familiar with this process, give him or her all the pieces for a puzzle, and see what he or she does with them.

• Talk to the baby about how God made a place for everything God created. Use language like "God made the stars and a place for the stars. God put stars in the sky!" or "God made the fish and a place for the fish. God put fish in the water!"

• As babies' skills progress, let them do puzzles with more pieces. Older walkers might even be challenged by giving them more pieces than there are spaces on the foam.

• Watch for signs of frustration, and give help and encouragement as needed, but allow babies as much independence as possible as they do this activity.

Maintenance Message

Store the foam flat to keep it properly shaped, and store the cookie cutters separately.

Other Notes

Sandpaper Blocks

Activity: *Babies will stack and build with these lightweight, textured blocks.*

Purpose: *To develop balance and creative thinking skills.*

Make-It Level: Medium preparation

Use-It Level: Low preparation

Materials Needed: For each block, you'll need two milk cartons of matching size, scissors, glue, and sandpaper.

Getting Ready

Collect and wash the milk cartons. You can get a lot of eight-ounce cartons by spending one lunch hour at your local school cafeteria (with permission, of course). Cut each of two cartons to the height you want the finished block to be, leaving the bottoms intact. Set one milk carton on its end, and slide the open end of the second carton inside. Push them together until they won't slide anymore. Apply glue to the entire outer surface of the block, and wrap sandpaper around it. When babies build with these blocks, the sandpaper holds the blocks together.

More Merriment

- Rub two blocks together in time to some cheerful praise music.
- Give the babies pieces of felt or yarn to stick on the sandpaper for a removable art project.

Sandpaper Blocks

How to Use This Toy

With Babies of All Ages:

• Allow the babies to freely explore and build with the blocks.

• Use the blocks to model number concepts when you are telling a story such as Jesus calling two disciples; Noah's animals, two by two; Noah's three sons; or five loaves and two fishes.

• Stick felt and yarn facial features on the blocks, and use them as story characters. A yarn mouth easily changes expression as events change during the story.

• Create a simple block pattern (such as side by side, or one on top of another), and encourage the baby to copy it.

• Build a tall tower, and knock it over. Because the blocks are covered with sandpaper, they tend not to go too far, especially if you use them on a carpet.

• Explore different sounds the blocks make when you bang them together or rub them together. Use them as musical instruments.

Maintenance Message

Confine these blocks to a specific area, and keep babies separated as they play to prevent them from accidentally scraping one another with the sandpaper.

Other Notes

Water-Ballet Bags

Activity: *Babies will control the action of the sparkling dancers in these squishy little bags.*

Purpose: *To give children a multisensory, independent-learning experience.*

Make-It Level: Low preparation

Use-It Level: Medium preparation

Materials Needed: For each Water-Ballet Bag, you'll need a gallon-sized resealable freezer bag (color-change seals are best for this activity), a small package of Mylar confetti, water, and masking tape.

Getting Ready

Empty the bag of confetti into the resealable bag. Add three inches of water in the bottom of the bag. Seal the bag. Open a little space, force almost all the air out, and then reseal tightly.

Lay the bag on a flat surface (either the floor or a table). With masking tape, secure the bag to the surface on all sides.

More Merriment

• Add food coloring to the bags to stimulate babies' vision with the color.

• Store the bags in the refrigerator for a cool experience, or add warm (not hot) water just before use.

• Use giant Mylar confetti. Add one big item along with the little ones, or use glitter instead of small confetti.

• Fill a bag one-quarter full with baby lotion, and leave the confetti out. As the baby presses on the bag, the underlying surface shows through, making pretty patterns.

• For a one- or two-time treat, put shaving cream in the bag, and let the babies squish the bag to discover what develops.

Water-Ballet Bags

How to Use This Toy

With Holders (three to seven months old)
and Crawlers (seven to twelve months old):

Tape the bag to the floor, and place a blanket beside it. Lay the baby on his or her tummy on the blanket. Encourage the baby to touch the bag. It makes an interesting sound, feels different than the blanket, and each touch sends the contents dancing. Babies who crawl will enjoy exploring how different movements affect the contents.

With Walkers (twelve to twenty-four months old):

• Mount the bag on the table. This activity offers many of the exploration benefits of a water table without the mess. Encourage babies to press with one finger, with their whole hand, gently, quickly, slowly—in as many different ways as you can model.

• Play praise music, and encourage the baby to make the contents of the bag dance praise to God. Then encourage the baby to bounce and shake his or her body to the music as well.

Maintenance Message

Store these bags with the seal up. They'll last indefinitely, but you can remove the water to change the temperature or otherwise vary the contents by opening the seal just a tiny bit.

Other Notes

Chapter 3

APPEALING ART

This chapter includes early art experiences and multisensory activities that have many different applications. All build artistic expression, but some do even more. Some build coordination skills. Others build problem-solving skills. Some are fun to eat. Yet all of them are a lot of fun for babies.

The activities in this chapter are based on experience. You can do every activity within these pages dozens of times. Babies never tire of opportunities for creative expression!

Here are ideas to get you started.

Fancy, Fruity Finger Paint

Activity: *Babies will use their fingers to paint one-of-a-kind pictures.*

Purpose: *To give babies an early multisensory experience in artistic expression.*

Make-It Level: Medium preparation

Use-It Level: High preparation

Materials Needed: A saucepan, a stove, measuring cups, a bowl, cornstarch, water, fruit-flavored gelatin (lighter colors have less stain potential), a wooden spoon, an unbreakable air-tight storage jar, wax paper or a table with a smooth surface, and art paper for printing (optional).

Getting Ready

Soften the fruit-flavored gelatin in one-quarter cup boiling water in the bowl. Set it aside. Measure one-half cup of cornstarch and three-quarters cup of cold water into the saucepan. Stir until smooth. Then stir in two cups of hot water. Cook over medium-high heat, stirring constantly, until the mixture becomes thick and translucent. Remove the mixture from the heat, and stir in the gelatin. Cool without refrigerating. You now have fancy, fruity finger paint.

More Merriment

• For a different textural experience, add one-quarter cup sand to the cooled mixture.

• Give babies other finger-painting experiences with one of the following supplies: pudding, yogurt, whipped cream, shaving cream, or baby lotion.

Fancy, Fruity Finger Paint

How to Use This Activity

With Babies of All Ages:

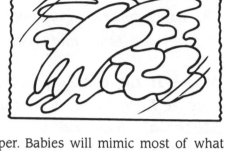

• Allow one or two babies to paint at a time.

• Protect the babies' clothing with oversized T-shirts. Have a damp towel or baby wipes at the work area for quick cleanup.

• Put about one tablespoon of the fancy, fruity finger paint on a piece of wax paper. Allow the baby to touch the mixture, and show him or her how it slides on the wax paper. Babies will mimic most of what you show them how to do.

• As the baby explores, thank God for fingers to feel the slippery paint; for noses to smell the yummy fruit smell; for eyes to see the pretty designs; and even for towels to wash it all off!

• When the baby's interest wanes, place a piece of art paper over the top and press down lightly to create a print to share with parents. This particular paint has an interesting appearance when it's dry.

• For another interesting experience, smear paint on a square of unbreakable plastic mirror, and let the baby wipe off a little paint at a time, revealing his or her image (be ready to wipe fingers after each stroke). It's similar to reverse portrait painting.

Maintenance Message

• Protect the work area by using two plastic tablecloths. Place one on the table and another one underneath it to protect the floor.

• Babies probably will taste this finger paint, which is nontoxic. However, discourage babies from ingesting large amounts of it.

Other Notes

Sticky Collages

Activity: Babies will create no-glue collages.

Purpose: To give babies tactile experience in using a sticky substance and creative expression.

Make-It Level: Low preparation

Use-It Level: Medium preparation

Materials Needed: Self-adhesive plastic shelf covering, scissors, masking tape, and a variety of lightweight items that fit with your theme. (See "Getting Ready" for items that go along with different themes.)

Getting Ready

Cut one twelve-inch square of self-adhesive shelf covering for each baby. Peel off the backing for one project at a time. Use masking tape to tape it to a table or wall sticky side up. Secure all the edges.

Select items to go along with one of the following teaching themes, or choose a theme of your own:

- God created plants—grass clippings, pine needles, flowers, leaves.
- God created animals—feathers, leather strips, synthetic fur, cutouts of critters.
- God created the earth—dirt, sand, potting soil.
- God created the sea—small shells, dried seaweed, fish cutouts.
- God made many shapes—cutouts of circles, squares, and triangles.
- God made many colors—multicolored paper scraps.

More Merriment

- Cut a piece of adhesive plastic large enough to cover the whole table, and let all the babies add to the collage.
- Use clear adhesive plastic, and add tissue paper or cellophane scraps to create the effect of a stained-glass window.
- Sticker art is the opposite of this activity. Babies will enjoy pulling stickers off a sheet and freely placing them on a paper plate. Loosen one edge of each sticker so babies can pull them off the backing by themselves. Office dots are an inexpensive treat.

Sticky Collages

How to Use This Activity

With Babies of All Ages:

• Let the baby touch and explore the stickiness of the paper.

• Hand the baby one item at a time to stick on the paper as you reinforce the teaching point.

• After the baby has the idea of sticking things on the paper, present the baby with several choices of items to stick on.

• If you are using clear adhesive plastic, fold the finished collage in half for easy transport. To hang the collage, put a twenty-four-inch piece of yarn on the fold line before sticking the edges together. Tie the ends of the yarn together. To make this art even more special, add a frame made of construction paper.

Maintenance Message

Work with one or two babies at a time to continuously remind them that the items should not be placed in their mouths.

Other Notes

Neat-Scoop Loops

Activity: *Babies will scoop and pour oat loop cereal.*

Purpose: *To give babies a chance to practice coordination and thinking skills.*

Make-It Level: Medium preparation

Use-It Level: Medium preparation

Materials Needed: A cardboard box (at least twelve inches by twenty inches, cut to three inches tall), two extra-large whipped-topping containers with lids, a plastic measuring cup or laundry detergent scoop, low-temperature hot glue and glue gun, poster putty, and oat loop cereal.

Getting Ready

Use the hot glue to glue the bottoms of both plastic containers to the inside of the cardboard box. Pour oat loops into one of the containers. Each time the activity is set up, put a ball of poster putty on each outside corner of the bottom of the box. Press the corners onto the table to hold the box firmly in place.

To store the activity, put all the cereal in one container and the scoop and the putty in the other container. Label the lids appropriately.

More Merriment

• Put cornmeal in the container with the oat loops. Use a mesh strainer instead of a scoop to remove the cereal. Show the babies how to shake all the cornmeal out before dumping the oat loops in the other container.

• Use an egg carton with happy-face dots in the bottom of each cup. Talk about sharing, and encourage the baby to put a little cereal in each of the egg cups. Older babies can put one loop in each cup of the egg cartons for a greater challenge.

Neat-Scoop Loops

How to Use This Activity

With Babies of All Ages:

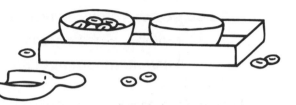

• Let babies practice scooping and pouring in one container first, keeping the lid on the second container. This tidy activity allows babies to engage in the fill-and-dump game they love and learn so much from without making a big mess.

• Remove the lid from the second container, and show the baby how to scoop from the full container and dump the contents into the empty container.

• When the baby gets good at the skill, introduce an egg carton with face stickers in the bottom of each cup. Have the baby put some oat loops in each of the egg cups. Talk about sharing by giving each of the friends in the egg cups part of the cereal. Talk about how it makes God happy when we share. It is this kind of gentle conversation that lets babies know God is part of our everyday lives.

• Introduce the concept of sifting by adding cornmeal to the oat loops. Give the baby a strainer, and show him or her how to get all of the cornmeal out before dumping the oat loops into the container.

Maintenance Message

Store the cereal in one covered container and the poster putty and scoops in the other. Use the lids to help you dump from one container without dumping the other.

Other Notes

Squeeze Art

Activity: *Babies will squeeze substances from soft-sided bottles.*
Purpose: *To give babies an opportunity to safely and to creatively explore an activity that is universally appealing, and to develop small motor strength and coordination.*

Make-It Level: Medium preparation
Use-It Level: Medium preparation
Materials Needed: One or more squeeze bottles (hair-coloring bottles from a beauty supply shop are perfect and inexpensive); equal parts of salt, flour, and water (about three to six tablespoons); food coloring or washable tempera; and cookie sheets.

Getting Ready

Mix equal parts of salt, flour, and water, starting with three tablespoons of each for each bottle. Add enough color from the food coloring or washable tempera to obtain the desired color. Put the mixture in the squeeze bottle, and put the lid on. Squeeze out a little. It should squeeze easily, but not run. If it's too thick, add water a few drops at a time. If it's too thin, add a teaspoon of equal parts of salt and flour at a time.

More Merriment

• Experiment with the size of the hole in the lid of the squeeze bottle.
• Make several different colors of squeeze paint.
• Try other combinations of squeezable paint and canvas: Jelly and bread, pudding and pound cake, finger paint (see recipe on page 48) and wax paper, or cheese sauce and crackers.

Squeeze Art

How to Use This Activity

With Babies of All Ages:

• Allow one or two babies to paint at a time.

• To protect babies' clothing, cover them with oversized T-shirts. Have a damp towel or baby wipes at the work area for quick cleanup.

• Put a cookie sheet on the work table.

• Show the baby how to hold the squeeze bottle with both hands and press to release the paint onto the cookie sheet. Let the baby explore what it takes to squeeze out a puddle and what it takes to squeeze out a line.

• Talk about the differences between squeezing lightly and squeezing hard.

• Encourage the baby to create a picture. Talk about how God gave babies strong hands to create beautiful things.

• If you have selected an edible paint and canvas, praise the child for creating his or her own snack, and thank God for yummy food to help our bodies grow stronger every day.

Maintenance Message

• Protect the work area by using two plastic tablecloths. Place one on the table and the other one underneath to protect the floor.

• If a baby can't make anything come out of the squeeze bottle, increase the size of the hole by cutting a tiny fraction of the nozzle away, or thin the paint with about a quarter of a teaspoon of water at a time.

Other Notes

Play Clay

Activity: *Babies will push and press one of these pliable clays.*
Purpose: *To provide babies with a soothing tactile experience.*

Make-It Level: Medium preparation
Use-It Level: Low preparation
Materials Needed: Airtight containers; plastic place mats; items to press into the clay such as large three-inch birthday candles, tongue depressors, plastic cookie cutters, or plastic spoons; and one of the following recipes, prepared ahead of time.

Edible Play Clay

One box cake mix
⅓ cup vegetable oil
3 tablespoons water

Mix well. Knead with your hands. If the mixture is too sticky or oily, add flour one tablespoon at a time. If the mixture is too dry, add one teaspoon of water at a time. This is a one-use mixture and should not be stored.

Soft Play Dough

1 cup flour	1 tablespoon oil
1 cup water	1 package unsweetened
½ cup salt	powdered drink mix
1 tablespoon cream of tartar	

Combine all ingredients in a medium-sized saucepan. Cook over high heat, stirring constantly, until dough is the desired consistency.

Soda Clay

1 cup cornstarch
2 cups baking soda
1 ¼ cups water
Food coloring

Combine all ingredients in a medium-sized saucepan. Cook over medium heat, stirring constantly, until the mixture is the consistency of dough.

Modeling Sand

1 cup sand	¾ cup hot water
1 teaspoon alum	Food coloring
(found in the spice aisle)	
½ cup cornstarch	

Mix dry ingredients. Add hot water, stirring vigorously to mix. Add food coloring. Cook over medium heat until the mixture thickens.

Getting Ready

Make one of the mixtures before class. Store it in an airtight container. Put out plastic place mats with a portion of play clay on each.

Working with one of the wonderfully squishy play clays can be a great stress buster for babies. Don't expect them to create any-

Dryer Lint Clay

3 cups dryer lint	3 drops oil of cloves or
⅔ cup flour	peppermint
2 cups water	

Mix lint and flour in a large saucepan. Stir in water a little at a time to prevent lumps. Add oil of cloves or peppermint. Cook over low heat, stirring constantly, until soft peaks form. Cool mixture on paper towels or newspaper.

thing. Babies (even as old as walkers) will not sculpt with the mixture. They'll just manipulate the material. They will enjoy pinching, prodding, and poking things into the play clay. Give them tongue depressors, birthday candles, plastic cookie cutters, or plastic spoons to use. (Supervise the babies closely because these items often will end up in their mouths.)

More Merriment

Babies may have fun with a mixture of two parts cornstarch to one part water poured on a foam plate. This mixture can't decide whether it's a solid or a liquid, and neither can the baby!

Play Clay

How to Use This Activity

With Babies of All Ages:

• Always play with clay on plastic place mats for quick cleanup and to provide boundaries when two or more babies are working in the same area.

• Show the baby how to poke one finger into the clay—then two, three, four fingers—and then the whole hand.

• Give the baby different quantities of the clay to explore, from a tiny pea-sized ball to the whole lump at once!

• Let babies use play kitchen utensils, such as plastic cookie cutters, birthday candles, plastic spoons, or craft sticks, to press into the clay.

Maintenance Message

Protect the work area by placing a plastic tablecloth under the table.

Other Notes

Jelly Bags

Activity: Babies will mix colors in this no-mess finger-paint activity.

Purpose: To give babies an opportunity to observe what happens when colors mix.

Make-It Level: Medium preparation

Use-It Level: Low preparation

Materials Needed: Two or three different colors of three-ounce boxes of gelatin for every four babies, prepared as directed; a pint-size resealable freezer bag for each baby; a quart-size resealable freezer bag for each baby; and masking tape.

Getting Ready

Put one portion of each color gelatin in each of the pint-size freezer bags. Squeeze out most of the air, and seal the bags as you go. Put a strip of masking tape across the top of each bag, and tape the pint-size bags to the inside of the quart-size bags. Remove the air, and seal the larger bags, too. Keep these in the refrigerator until you're ready to use them.

More Merriment

Replace the gelatin with corn syrup colored with food coloring or tempera paint. Store at room temperature.

Jelly Bags

How to Use This Activity

With Babies of All Ages:

• Encourage babies to use one finger to swirl around the gelatin in their bags, like finger painting.

• Point out how the colors are different and how they look when they mix together.

• Sing this song to the tune of "Did You Ever See a Lassie?" as the babies play:

Only God can make the colors, the colors, the colors,
Only God can make the colors that swirl round and round.
There are red, blue and yellow, and green, orange and purple.
Swirl them all together, and then they look brown!

• Hang several of the bags in the window to see the sun shining through.

• Even after the colors are muddy (if you used three colors, especially), babies will enjoy the feel of the squishy bags in their hands.

Maintenance Message

After babies are done playing, squeeze the gelatin into cups for a fun and tasty treat.

Other Notes

Chapter 4
COZY CORNERS

Creating a cozy nursery not only provides love and support for babies, but it also creates a space for maximum learning. In this chapter, you'll find plans for walls, floors, windows, and doors that will grab babies' attention and keep nursery operation running smoothly—even at changing time!

Let these ideas spark your imagination. Design freely, based on the needs and interests of your babies and families. Get multiple church committees involved in the process of decorating the nursery, and they will begin to feel connected to nursery ministry, even if they don't crawl on the floor with the babies.

Four of the ideas in this chapter focus on fun-zone rugs. These include a resting rug, a reading rug, a puzzle rug, and a road rug. Consider which rug would fit your situation best—or see if you can create more than one.

Here are ideas to get you started.

Wonderful, Whimsical Window Art

Activity: *Babies will identify and praise God for items in brightly colored temporary window murals.*

Purpose: *To provide an easily changeable, unique gallery for seasonal themes or teaching points.*

Make-It Level: Medium preparation

Use-It Level: Low preparation

Materials Needed: Simple art designs copied onto transparencies (get started with objects from the mural transparency found on p. 64), white butcher paper, masking tape, dry-erase markers, overhead projector, foam paintbrushes, and washable tempera paint.

Getting Ready

Cover the window frame with white butcher paper, leaving the glass exposed. Hold the paper in place with masking tape. Project the images you want to paint onto the window, carefully checking the placement. Use the dry-erase marker to outline the images. Then paint the images with the washable tempera paint. The outlines can be easily wiped away with a tissue.

You can eliminate the need for butcher paper and overhead transparencies if you draft a talented volunteer to create a scene freehand. Change the scene or individual elements of the scene to match the seasons or your teaching theme.

More Merriment

• Leave some animal or flower faces "open" so that people on the other side of the window can frame their faces to entertain the babies!

• Create translucent art on the windows by coloring with the dry-erase markers. Don't let babies touch this; it smudges easily.

• For real fun, let the babies take a turn with the paintbrush!

Wonderful, Whimsical Window Art

How to Use This Activity

With Babies of All Ages:

• Use a flashlight to point to individual images. Help the baby to name the objects you highlight.

• Have a "Pointer Parade of Praise." Let the baby point to a picture, and then praise God aloud for it. Babies will enjoy clapping and cheering their praises.

• Put a three-dimensional character into the scene. Bounce a stuffed bunny along, or let a lamb rest in the pasture.

Maintenance Message

The window mural can easily be removed by wiping it off with a damp cloth.

Other Notes

Parents' Peekaboo, One-Way Mirror

Activity: *Parents will be able to unobtrusively observe their children at any time through a peekaboo mirror.*

Purpose: *Satisfy parents' need to check up on babies without causing disruption to your nursery.*

Make-It Level: High preparation

Use-It Level: None

Materials Needed: A twelve-inch by twelve-inch square of one-way see-through safety mirror, eight twelve-inch strips of corner molding to hold the mirror in place from both sides, a saw to cut a hole in the outer door, nails to hold the molding in place, and a hammer.

Getting Ready

Receive approval from all the appropriate committees in your church before starting this project because it will permanently alter the nursery door. It is probably best to enlist the help of a glazier or experienced carpenter from the congregation.

Cut a 12 1/4-inch square in the door, horizontally centered, with the bottom edge no higher than four feet from the bottom of the door so that it's easy to see infants playing on the floor. Nail the molding in place around the edges of the hole on one side of the door. Slip the mirror in place from the other side with the mirror side facing into the nursery and window side facing out. Hold the mirror in place, sandwich-style, by nailing the remaining molding strips around the hole in the other side of the door.

Soon after you install the mirror, send home a letter to help families understand why it is important to use this mirror rather than enter the nursery at unscheduled times. You may complete and photocopy the letter on page 66 to send home, or use it as a model for your own letter.

More Merriment

Ask someone (other than a parent of a baby) to use the peekaboo, one-way mirror when you're not expecting it. Have that person tell you what he or she observes and give you feedback on the observation and the use of the mirror. This can help you make any necessary improvements.

Parents' Peekaboo, One-Way Mirror

Dear Parents:

We want you to be aware of what's happening with your baby in the nursery, and we want you to always feel welcome. We also want your baby and the others in the nursery to have a warm, happy, and peaceful experience each time they are here.

Unpredictable parent visits sometimes interfere with a baby's ability to settle in and feel comfortable in this setting. A baby who has already overcome a bout of separation anxiety can become exhausted when he or she is left by a parent a second time (even if the parent is not his or her own).

To make sure you can check on your baby at any time without causing any undue anxiety, we have installed a "Peekaboo Mirror." It is located _____. This mirror will allow you to peek into the nursery and observe the children at play without them ever knowing you are there. You'll be reassured your child is safe and happy while the babies will be able to continue their pursuits without disruption.

Your baby's comfort is our greatest concern. We want your baby to come to love his or her time in the church nursery and to come to know the Savior in whose name we gather.

If I can answer any questions or be of help to you in any way, please call me at

_____.

_____

Nursery Coordinator

A Little Door of My Own

Activity: *Babies will happily enter the nursery through a kid-sized door.*

Purpose: *To have babies enter the nursery with a confident "I-can-do-it-myself" attitude, helping the parents release their babies with confidence, as well.*

Make-It Level: High preparation

Use-It Level: Medium preparation

Materials Needed: Security gate that has a tension rod and swinging door; poster boards; duct tape; baby animal and flower photos from old calendars, seed catalogs and magazines; scissors; glue; hole punch; heavy yarn; yarn needle; fabric glue; twenty-four by forty-two-inch fabric printed with sky and cloud print design; and a tension rod.

Getting Ready

Cut the poster boards so that the boards can completely cover a security gate. Cut out the collected pictures, and glue them onto the poster boards to reinforce a Creation theme. Punch holes around the perimeter of the boards two inches from each edge, three inches apart. Loop pieces of duct tape on the back of each poster board, and fasten the poster boards to each side of the gate, pressing the sides together to hold them in place. Use the yarn to lace the poster boards to the edges of the gate.

Next create a curtain. Fold the bottom edge of the fabric up one inch, and use fabric glue to hold it in place. Fold the top edge over three inches, and secure it with fabric glue to form a pocket. Slide the tension rod into the pocket. Position the tension rod in the doorway so that the bottom of the fabric touches the top of the gate. This will allow parents to see over the top and converse with teachers or volunteers.

More Merriment

Change the door theme to coordinate with holiday seasons. For a more permanent kid-sized door, have a carpenter cut your door in half above the doorknob to make a "Dutch door." Purchase a second set of door hinges and doorknob mountings. Mount the hinges so that each half of the door has hinges at the top and bottom. Keep the top closed, and open the bottom to allow the baby to walk or crawl in. The bottom half of the door can be decorated with the poster boards as described above. Attach the poster boards with duct tape.

A Little Door of My Own

How to Use This Door

With Babies of All Ages:

• Move the curtain to one side to receive younger babies.

• Choose one of the following songs or chants to welcome the baby to the nursery:

Welcome to Your Church

(to the tune of "If You're Happy and You Know It")

Welcome to your church, come on in!
Welcome to your church, come on in!
We'll learn and pray and play,
And have some fun today!
Welcome to your church, come on in!

Knock- Knock Chant
Knock, knock...
Peek in...
Open the latch, and put on a grin.
[Child's name] **has come to church today**
To learn about Jesus. Now let's go play!

Oh, Look!

(to the tune of "Oh, Dear! What Can the Matter Be?")

Oh, look! Here comes my baby friend,
Oh, look! Here comes my baby friend,
Oh, look! Here comes my baby friend,
I am so glad that you're here.
Walk through the door and give me a little smile,
Walk through the door and give me a little grin,
Walk through the door and give me a little hug,
I am so glad that you're here.

Use this song with a fluffy puppet greeter.

Other Notes

My Own Door With Wall Mural

Activity: *Babies will identify the nursery entrance as they approach their class.*

Purpose: *To help babies recognize and identify with their own special place in God's house.*

Make-It Level: High preparation

Use-It Level: Low to medium preparation

Materials Needed: Mural design (from pages 70 and 71) copied onto transparencies, overhead projector, pencil, acrylic paints, paint trays, and foam brushes.

Getting Ready

Receive approval from all the appropriate committees in your church before starting this project because it will permanently alter the nursery door.

Project a design on the nursery door and surrounding wall. Trace the lines of the design on the door and wall with a pencil so they can be erased if necessary. If the area outside the nursery door doesn't allow you to project the images at the proper size, project the design onto butcher paper, and transfer it onto the wall with graphite paper. Fill in the outline with acrylic paint.

Send home a letter to introduce the mural to families and to encourage them to use it with their babies. You may photocopy the letter on page 72 to send home, or use it as a model for your own letter.

More Merriment

• Instead of painting in the outlines, use textured fabric glue-ons so babies can interact with the scene. Use vinyl reptiles and amphibians, fuzzy mammals, feathers on birds, textured spray paint, or artificial turf on the ground. Create fluffy clouds by sponging white paint over the background color with an up-and-down wrist motion.

• Hang Christmas lights around the mural to attract attention.

• Use chalkboard paint (see your paint-supply dealer) over a portion of the mural to create a chalkboard. Use colored chalk on the chalkboard portion of the door to note special events or parent updates, such as: "We welcome new baby Paul, born to Jim and Sarah Marshall last Tuesday," "Today's volunteers are Rosemary and Connie—Thanks for investing in our babies," or "Today's toddler snack is peanut butter and crackers."

My Own Door With Wall Mural

Dear Parents:

As you approach the nursery, take time to point out some of the details on the wall mural outside the door. This wall has some unique things to explore together. It's a hands-on wall, so touch items you pass. Say "Good morning" to the characters. Point out to children that these things are part of the wonderful world God created for our enjoyment.

On the way out, go through a similar goodbye ritual. It may take a few minutes extra, but you will be building a love of God's house to last a lifetime.

Your Nursery Staff

Dear Parents:

As you approach the nursery, take time to point out some of the details on the wall mural outside the door. This wall has some unique things to explore together. It's a hands-on wall, so touch items you pass. Say "Good morning" to the characters. Point out to children that these things are part of the wonderful world God created for our enjoyment.

On the way out, go through a similar goodbye ritual. It may take a few minutes extra, but you will be building a love of God's house to last a lifetime.

Your Nursery Staff

Resting Rug

Activity: *Babies will use the designated area for resting and relaxing.*

Purpose: *To designate a specific space that will signal to babies that it's time to rest.*

Make-It Level: Medium preparation

Use-It Level: Low preparation

Materials Needed: Blue carpet remnant at least four feet by four feet, four bed pillows covered with plastic cases, four washable pillowcases (a cloud design is one idea), four strips of heavy-duty Velcro hook and loop fasteners, fabric glue, scissors, stuffed animals, additional pillows, and receiving blankets.

Getting Ready

Choose a corner area out of the traffic flow and not too near the toys. Lay the blue carpet on the floor. Measure and cut strips of Velcro to correspond to the size of the pillowcases. Mount one side of each strip of Velcro about one foot from the baseboard on each wall. Using fabric glue, attach the other sides of the Velcro strips to each pillowcase. (Note: Before attaching the Velcro to the pillowcases, arrange the pillows against the wall to determine the appropriate placement.) Place a pillow in each pillowcase, and attach the pillows to the wall. Put a few stuffed animals, throw pillows, and blankets around the area.

More Merriment

• Play soft classical or instrumental music in this corner. A lot of classical music was composed for church use.

• Designate a separate area nearby as an eating area. Include a snack table and a rocking chair to give babies a bottle. Having a separate eating area will keep babies from taking bottles and snacks around the room.

Resting Rug

How to Use This Rug

With Holders (three to seven months old):

Sit with babies on the rug, or place their baby seats on the rug. Babies can face the wall to shut out the stimulation of the rest of the room. Sing this quiet lullaby to the tune of "Jesus Loves Me":

> *Jesus loves me when I rest,*
> *Quiets me and I am blessed.*
> *I am safely in his care.*
> *He will hear my every prayer.*

Remember to never leave a baby propped with a bottle.

With Crawlers (seven to twelve months old):

Let babies sit on the rug, lie down with a blanket, or lean against one of the wall pillows. As you pat or stroke these little bundles of energy, pray aloud: **Thank you, God, for quiet places to rest and relax.** Model quiet humming along with instrumental or classical music. Keep talking to a minimum in this corner. Children can hold their own bottles in this area.

With Walkers (twelve to twenty-four months old):

Let walkers know this is a no-walk zone. Everyone sits or lies down on the resting rug. Whisper this chant as part of welcoming them to the resting rug:

> *Lie down on the resting rug and curl up like a little bug,*
> *Here's a place where you can be so quiet.*
> *I'll give you a little hug, give the blanket one big tug,*
> *Sneak up here beside me, let's be quiet!* (Shhhhh!)

Calm small children by patting or rubbing their backs.

Maintenance Message

Pull the pillows off the wall, remove the pillowcases, and wash them inside out whenever they become soiled.

Other Notes

Reading Rug

Activity: *Babies will use the designated area for reading and looking at books.*

Purpose: *To designate a specific space for reading.*

Make-It Level: Medium preparation

Use-It Level: Low preparation

Materials Needed: A four-foot by three-foot rug, an eight-foot strip of Velcro hook and loop fasteners, tacky glue, crib mattress, crib sheet, pencil, rectangular plastic basket, and baby board books.

Getting Ready

Choose a space, and place the rug lengthwise against the wall. Cut the Velcro strip in half, and glue two strips lengthwise across the bottom side of the crib mattress six inches from each edge. Position the rug against the wall. Place the mattress against the wall with the Velcro against the wall, and mark the position of the Velcro with a pencil. Glue the two matching strips of Velcro on the wall. Put the crib sheet on the mattress, and press the mattress against the wall so the Velcro connects. Place baby board books in a basket. Center the basket against the mattress.

More Merriment

Remove the mattress from the wall, and set it up as a supervised jumping area in another part of the room. Make sure the area around the mattress is free of anything that an infant can fall on, and have an adult at the mattress to closely supervise the jumpers. Allow only one or two at a time. Remove the sheet before allowing children to step on the mattress.

Reading Rug

How to Use This Rug

With Holders (three to seven months old):

Sit on the rug together. Turn the pages of a board book. Point to different parts of the picture. Speak slowly.

With Crawlers (seven to twelve months old):

Let babies turn the pages of a board book themselves. Encourage babies to repeat the words you read. Ask babies what they see in the pictures.

With Walkers (twelve to twenty-four months old):

• The mattress can be removed from the wall so babies can put the book on the mattress and prop their elbows on the mattress while the rest of their bodies rest on the floor.

• Keep age-appropriate Bibles stored in a separate area. (These Bibles often are storybook Bibles.) Bring out these Bibles at a special time when all of the older babies are gathered on the reading rug. Emphasize the special nature of the Bibles. Teach babies how to turn the pages carefully. Teach the name "Bible," and talk about how this special book is a present from God, just for them.

Sing this song to the tune of "Did You Ever See A Lassie?"

Oh, it's time to read the Bible, the Bible, the Bible.
Oh, it's time to read the Bible, God's special book.
I turn the pages and look at the pictures.
Oh, it's time to read the Bible, God's special book.

Maintenance Message

Remove the mattress cover for easy washing.

Other Notes

Puzzle Rug

Activity: *Babies will use the designated area for doing puzzles.*

Purpose: *To designate a specific space for stimulating infants through puzzles.*

Make-It Level: High preparation

Use-It Level: Low to medium preparation

Materials Needed: Carpet remnants or samples in various colors but all the same size, felt-tipped marking pen, carpet knife, fabric paint, and duct tape.

Getting Ready

With the felt-tipped marking pen draw simple shapes on the back of the carpet remnants, such as a square, triangle, circle, and rectangle. Using a carpet knife, cut around the outline of the shape from the back side, keeping the outline in one piece and the shape in another piece. Cover the edges with duct tape to prevent unraveling and sharp edges. Paint each cutout a different color than the rug you cut it from.

Use duct tape to attach the large carpet pieces to the floor, piecing them together to form one rectangular rug area. Don't tape down the shapes that were cut out. The shapes can be removed and replaced for fun.

More Merriment

Put on praise music, and have each baby who can do so stand on a different shape and praise God to the music.

Puzzle Rug

How to Use This Rug

With Holders (three to seven months old):

Let babies lie on the rugs and hold the pieces, or hold a baby and move his or her hand around the edges of each piece as you say the name of each shape.

With Crawlers (seven to twelve months old):

Sit with babies on the floor with the puzzle pieces removed. Let them explore the holes in the rugs. Help them identify each shape. Then give them one piece at a time. Help the babies identify the colors and place the pieces.

With Walkers (twelve to twenty-four months old):

Place all the puzzle pieces in the center of the rug. Let the babies try to place the pieces, or give them specific directions to follow based on color and shape, such as, "Pick up the red circle."

Maintenance Message

Remove the pieces, and set them aside before vacuuming this rug.

Other Notes

Road Rug

Activity: *Babies will use the designated area to stimulate their imagination and learn about labels of different items.*

Purpose: *To designate a specific space for playing with cars and trucks.*

Make-It Level: Medium preparation

Use-It Level: Low preparation

Materials Needed: A three-foot by three-foot looped, low-pile carpet remnant; masking tape; acrylic paint; stencil brushes; foam meat tray for paint; and push cars and trucks.

Getting Ready

Plan a simple road design. On the carpet remnant, outline the streets with masking tape. Fill in the road areas with dark paint, and then remove the masking tape. Add a white, dotted line down the center of the roads to designate lanes. Decorate the outlying areas with painted-on grass, houses, and trees.

More Merriment

Create road rugs from different parts of the country. For example, create an urban road rug with skyscrapers along the roads; a zoo rug on which the road weaves through zoo animals; a construction rug with construction vehicles; a rural rug with farm equipment and farm animals; or a suburban rug with houses, driveways, and parks.

Road Rug

How to Use This Rug

With Holders (three to seven months old):

Lay the baby on his or her tummy on the carpet. Hold a car in the baby's hand. Help him or her to push the car. Make lots of sound effects for fun.

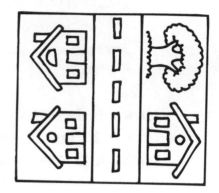

With Crawlers (seven to twelve months old):

Show babies how to keep a car on the road. Give them lots of praise as they control the action. Say: **God wants us to stay on God's path, too.**

With Walkers (twelve to twenty-four months old):

Encourage lots of verbalization as small children guide their cars and trucks. Ask questions about where they are going, such as, "Are you on your way to church?" "Are you going to grandma's house to give her hugs and kisses?" and "Who are you taking to Sunday school today in your bright red car?"

Maintenance Message

Spray each car with disinfectant solution after each play session.

Other Notes

Activity-Wall Train

Activity: *An activity wall can combine a number of displays to create interesting items for babies to interact with and look at.*

Purpose: *To create a wall with a variety of stimulating activities for babies.*

Make-It Level: Medium to high preparation

Use-It Level: Low to medium preparation

Materials Needed: Completed activity boards (see "Learn-About-Me, Fun Flannel Board" on page 82, "Baby-Safe Bulletin Board" on page 83, "Mirror, Mirror, Who's That?" on page 84, "Magical Magnet Board" on page 85, and "Baby Chalkboard" on page 86), paint, paintbrush, wooden rulers, scissors, large paper plate, and push pins.

Getting Ready

Choose and construct the panels you want to use, and mount them on a wall, joining them together as part of a giant activity train. Make each train car by painting a four-inch border around each frame. Join the cars with wooden rulers painted black and mounted on the wall. To make a stencil for the wheels, cut out the center of a large paper plate, being careful to keep the cut-out shape perfectly round. Use push pins to fasten the plate into position under each rectangle, and paint two wheels on each car.

More Merriment

Have the baby wear a baby-sized engineer hat while visiting your activity-wall train.

Learn-About-Me, Fun Flannel Board

Activity: Babies will have fun arranging facial features.

Purpose: To develop small motor skills and learn the parts of faces.

Make-It Level: Medium preparation

Use-It Level: Low preparation

Materials Needed: For the flannel board, you need a sixteen-inch by twenty-inch acrylic-plastic poster frame with slide-off plastic edges (available at art supply stores), a piece of felt eighteen inches by twenty-two inches, scissors, tacky glue, a foam brush, and plastic mirror mounts with screws. For the felt cutouts, you need appropriate colors of felt to make various skin tones and facial features.

Getting Ready

Remove the plastic edges from the poster frame, and discard the cardboard backing. Cut square notches one inch deep into all four corners of the felt. Use a foam brush to cover the acrylic with tacky glue. Place the felt on the acrylic, smoothing out bubbles. The felt should stick out one inch on all sides, and notches should line up at the corners. When the glue is dry, fold excess felt over the edges to the back. Slide on the plastic edges. Mount the flannel board on a wall with the mirror clips.

Cut oval head shapes and facial features from the felt.

More Merriment

Make felt paper-doll-style figures and clothing, such as pants, skirts, shirts, shoes, hats, and so on. Make the figures and clothing as large as possible. Keep each paper-doll set in an envelope, and display only one set at a time.

Baby-Safe Bulletin Board

Activity: *Babies will touch and admire images displayed in bulletin boards mounted on a wall at their eye level.*

Purpose: *To provide a visual display area that babies can safely explore on their own because no pins, tacks, or staples are required.*

Make-It Level: Medium preparation

Use-It Level: Medium preparation

Materials Needed: For each bulletin board, you'll need an eighteen-inch by twenty-four-inch acrylic-plastic poster frame with slide-off plastic edges (available at art supply stores), and eight plastic mirror mounts with screws. For the bulletin-board displays, you'll need sheets of eighteen-inch by twenty-four-inch poster board or construction paper, children's art, magazine photos, and a glue stick or tape.

Getting Ready

Remove the plastic edges from the poster frame. Discard the cardboard backing, and attach the frame to the wall with two mirror mounts on each side of the frame, four inches from each corner. Mount the poster frame just above the baseboard, so even the crawlers can see it.

Create a display board by gluing pictures of children's art and magazine photos on the poster board. For more visual interest, add a border around the edges.

Loosen the screws on the mirror mounts at the top and on one side of the poster frame just enough to twist the clamps, releasing the acrylic cover. Slide the acrylic cover out, and slip the display board into place. Replace the acrylic cover, twist the mirror clamps back over the edge of the cover, and tighten the screws.

More Merriment

Create a bulletin board next to your changing station too. Experiment with colors and patterns, such as a black-and-white checkerboard background. Slide a single baby cutout into a scene. Ask one of your little observers to "Find the baby!"

Mirror, Mirror, Who's That?

Activity: *Babies will look at themselves in the mirror.*

Purpose: *To let babies delight in discovering how they appear.*

Make-It Level: Medium preparation

Use-It Level: No preparation

Materials Needed: A sixteen-inch by twenty-inch poster frame with removable plastic edges, a sixteen-inch by twenty-inch acrylic mirror that is 1/8 inch thick, and four plastic mirror mounts with screws.

Getting Ready

Slide edges from the frame, and discard the cardboard backing. Replace the clear acrylic with the mirrored acrylic. Mount the mirror with four mirror mounts, two centered on each side.

More Merriment

• Play "Show Me." Ask babies to show you a happy face, a sad face, a silly face, a waving hand, and so forth. Babies will gain experience in following directions, and it's fun for babies to watch their own responses.

• Play "God Made." Say to the baby: **God made your eyes. Show me your eyes. Point to your eyes in the mirror!** Continue naming facial features and body parts, encouraging the baby to identify each.

Maintenance Message

Clean the acrylic mirror with a soft cloth and a solution of one part isopropyl alcohol to three parts water. Do not use ammonia products; they eventually will cause small cracks to form in the acrylic.

Magical Magnet Board

Activity: *Babies can stick baby-sized shapes on the wall, and the shapes won't fall off.*

Purpose: *To promote manual dexterity while learning shapes and colors.*

Make-It Level: Medium preparation

Use-It Level: Low preparation

Materials Needed: For the magnet board, you'll need a drill, a sixteen-inch by twenty-inch cookie sheet, and four screws. For the magnet shapes, you'll need felt markers, flat foam sheets in bright colors, scissors, and self-stick magnet sheets.

Getting Ready

Drill a hole in each corner of the cookie sheet, and mount the sheet into the wall with screws. With a marker, draw shapes at least three inches across on the foam sheets. Make squares, circles, triangles, rectangles, and so on, and cut them out.

Place a flat foam shape on a self-stick magnet sheet and trace around it with a marker. Cut out the magnet shape. Peel the protective paper from the magnet shape, and press the foam shape onto it.

More Merriment

Collect photos of babies and baby animals from magazines, greeting cards, or old calendars. Cover with clear contact paper. Cut heads and bodies apart. Attach a sheet magnet to each piece. If you have photos of your babies' heads, make magnets of those too. Babies have fun putting the correct head and body together, or laughing at the incongruities of unmatched heads and bodies.

Baby Chalkboard

Activity: *Babies can make chalkboard scribbles.*

Purpose: *To develop small-muscle coordination and a sense of appropriate place to draw with chalk.*

Make-It Level: Medium preparation

Use-It Level: No preparation

Materials Needed: A sixteen-inch by twenty-inch Masonite board, four plastic mirror mounts with screws, chalkboard paint, a foam brush, and sidewalk chalk.

Getting Ready

Paint the Masonite board with chalkboard paint. After the paint dries, mount the board on the wall with mirror mounts, centering mirror mounts on each edge.

More Merriment

Expect and encourage large scribbles. As babies become more familiar with the process, show them how to draw lines and dots. Always keep the drawing time simple and fun.

Maintenance Message

Sidewalk chalk will wash off your walls with window spray and a soft cloth.

Chapter 5
ANGEL AIDS

Your babies are blessed with a heavenly host of cradle rockers and diaper changers. The volunteers who staff the nursery are precious messengers of God's love. Give them all the help you can so they can perform their tasks with grace and style.

The items in this section will give your volunteers and workers tools for their own use. Undoubtedly, you'll find many other ways to appreciate them, but a golden start is to provide them with equipment that makes their jobs just a little easier.

Here are suggestions to get you started.

Shoulder Apron

Summary: *These tidy cover-ups protect volunteers' vulnerable shoulder areas and provide a soft touch for tiny cheeks.*

Make-It Level: Medium preparation

Use-It Level: Low preparation

Materials Needed: Two soft terry cloth or velour dish towels approximately twelve inches by twenty-two inches, measuring tape, a marking pen, a sewing machine, and thread or fabric glue.

Getting Ready

Place towels with right sides together. On the top long edge, measure in five inches from one corner, and mark it with a small X. Measure two inches from the corner on the other side, and mark it with a small X. Sew a one-inch-deep seam from each upper corner to the X on either side. Turn the towels right side out. Fold the towels in half with the long seam in the front and the short seam in back.

To use the apron, the worker will put his or her head through the hole, placing the long seam in front. This apron covers both shoulders. To make a higher neckline in front, slide the long seam toward the back. The material (either terry cloth or velour) will hold the apron in place against most fabrics.

More Merriment

Have a lot of these on hand. Workers can change them quickly and easily as soon as they become soiled.

Shoulder Apron

How to Use This Helper

With Babies of All Ages:

• Protect your Sunday clothes, jewelry, and babies' delicate cheeks with these easy to wear mini-aprons that take special care of your shoulders. If a baby drools or spits up, change the apron with one hand, and never miss a beat.

• Sing this song to the tune of the chorus of the golden oldie, "Put Your Head on My Shoulder":

> **Rest your cheek on my shoulder, ooh-ooh-ooh-ooh**
> **Let me rock you now, baby,**
> **Let me tell you how, baby,**
> **Jesus loves you, little child.**

• Talk to the baby about how soft the apron feels.
Say: **Thank you, God, for soft, clean shoulders to rest our heads on.**

Maintenance Message

Wash these shoulder aprons in fragrance-free detergent with a little all-fabric bleach.

Other Notes

Baby Directory

Summary: *This quick-reference guide will give new and experienced workers important information about every baby in the nursery.*

Make-It Level: Low preparation

Use-It Level: Medium preparation

Materials Needed: An information page for each baby (photocopied from page 91), film and camera (instant-type cameras work well), plastic photo pages, and your nursery manual.

Getting Ready

Photocopy a supply of the baby directory page (p. 91). When a baby is enrolled, ask the parents to fill out the form on-site. Take a picture of the baby with his or her parents, and slip it into a photo pocket. Place the photo page in the nursery manual opposite the information page. This way, you can see the picture and information at a glance. Consider taking pictures of anyone else authorized to pick up the baby from the nursery. Even if you have a tagging system for pick-up, this can be a valuable tool for every worker.

More Merriment

• Update the photos every three months with a family picture day. Send out a mailing to publicize the day, and strive to have every baby in attendance.

• Present the photos to parents as a gift when the baby graduates from the nursery.

• Order double prints to start a nursery yearbook. Place the yearbook where the entire congregation can look at it periodically and watch the babies grow. These yearbooks become priceless records as babies graduate from the nursery.

Baby Directory

Vital Information

Baby's name: _____

Birth date: _____

Parents' names: _____

People authorized to pick up the baby: _____

Where parents are likely to be found during nursery hours: _____

_____

Baby's Preferences

Bottle formula:_____

Known allergies: _____

Food: _____

Blanket: _____

Activities:_____

Favorite toy: _____

Regular nap time: _____

Favorite song: _____

Best method to calm when crying:_____

Words used for toilet training:_____

Other Notes

Pocket Belt

Summary: *This easy-to-wear pocket belt allows workers to keep necessities such as tissues, bottles, and pacifiers out of babies' reach and frees up their hands for important tasks such a giving babies an extra loving touch.*

Make-It Level: Medium preparation

Use-It Level: None

Materials Needed: A square pot holder with a loop on one side (not at the corner), a mitt-shaped pot holder with a loop, a needle, thread, and a one-inch-wide web belt with a two-ring fastener (available in the women's fashion accessories department).

Getting Ready

Fold the square pot holder in half with the side having the loop facing up. Sew sides together, leaving the top with the loop open to form a small pocket. Slide the sewn pot holder and mitt pot holder onto the web belt. Store tissues in the small pocket and bottles in the mitt pot holder.

More Merriment

• Sew a second small pocket for pacifiers. Make one for each baby, and write names on the outside with fabric paint. Launder these little pockets with the crib bedding.

Pocket Belt

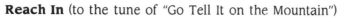

How to Use This Helper

With Babies of All Ages:

• Put this handy belt on over your clothes when you first arrive.

• This is the nursery worker's answer to needing another pair of hands. Carry an infant's bottle while you hold a toddler's hand, or make sure you are never far from tissues.

• Teach older babies to reach into your pockets by invitation for things they need when you have your hands full. Make this your invitation song:

Reach In (to the tune of "Go Tell It on the Mountain")

There's a tissue in my pocket,
Reach on in, and pull it out.
There's a tissue in my pocket,
And you may pull it out.

Substitute the name of whatever you are carrying for the word "tissue."

• To use this helper in a less utilitarian way, hide small toys or treats in the pockets. Play the game using this little chant:

God made a pocket inside the kangaroo.
Here are my little pockets,
I've got something just for you!

Maintenance Message

Remove the pot holders for frequent washing.

Other Notes

Boo-Boo Bags

Summary: *Stock up on these convenient, colorful, disposable ice packs, great for baby boo-boos or teething soothers.*

Make-It Level: Low preparation

Use-It Level: No preparation

Materials Needed: Gelatin, water, snack-sized resealable plastic bags, and three-inch-wide mailing tape.

Getting Ready

Make gelatin using the amount of hot water called for in the box directions but only half of the cold water. Fill the resealable plastic bags with one-half cup of the gelatin mixture. Remove most of the air, and seal the bags. Cover the opening with a strip of mailing tape folded over both sides of the bag. Store these bags in the refrigerator or freezer.

More Merriment

To use the bag as a teether, place the bag inside several other bags.

Boo-Boo Bags

How to Use This Helper
With Babies of All Ages:

> ## Our "Boo-Boo" Bags
> ## are located
> _____.

• To use Boo-Boo Bags as teethers, let babies hold them themselves. Make sure each bag is inside multiple bags to ensure that the gelatin won't leak.

• To use Boo-Boo Bags for minor injuries, hold the baby in your lap, and hold the bag against the baby's injury for the count of five. Then remove the bag for the count of ten before repeating. Never continuously hold a frozen object on a baby's delicate skin.

• Encourage the baby to notice the pretty color and temperature of the bag as a distraction from the pain. Older babies can be encouraged to count along with you as you count time on and time off.

• Follow the nursery policy and procedure for parental notification of injury.

Maintenance Message
Promptly dispose of any bag that comes in contact with bodily fluids.

Other Notes

Angel Quick Fixes

Summary: *Tips on how to keep the nursery in tip-top shape.*

Make-It Level: Low preparation

Use-It Level: Medium preparation

Materials Needed: Tube socks, fabric paint, plastic storage containers with tight-fitting lids, toothbrush cup holders, bleach, water, isopropyl alcohol, and window cleaner.

Angel Feet

• Encourage workers to shed their shoes to avoid accidental injury to babies on the floor. Purchase a large quantity of tube socks, and use fabric paint designs on the bottom to act as grippers. Workers can remove the socks after use, and the socks can be washed with the bedding.

Angel Storage

• To create extra storage areas for purses, shoes, or Bibles, use plastic storage containers with tight-fitting lids to keep little hands out. These containers can serve as baby height benches or table-play areas.

Angel Drinks

• Purchase toothbrush cup holders to hang on a wall out of babies' reach. Workers can put their coffee or other drinks here, where the drinks are unlikely to get tipped over.

Angel Cleaning

• Keep the following spray cleaning solutions on hand for quick clean-ups. For disinfecting: Mix one part bleach to ten parts water. For cleaning plastic and acrylic: Mix one part isopropyl alcohol to three parts water. Be sure to clean any unbreakable mirrors with this solution because ammonia products (such as window cleaner) eventually will cause small cracks to form in the acrylic.

The Warm and Wonderful

CHURCH NURSERY

Manual for:

Church Address: _____

_____

Church Phone: _____

Nursery Coordinator: _____

Appendix B: A Nursery Mission Statement

Do you have a mission statement for your nursery? A mission statement helps identify your vision and can ensure that everyone in your nursery knows its purpose. Think and pray about the following questions as you develop a nursery mission statement, and then give workers concrete suggestions for communicating the mission frequently.

- What do you want for babies?
- What do you want for parents?
- What do you want for workers and volunteers?
- What do you believe about the relationship between God and babies?
- What do you believe about the relationship between the church and babies?

Summarize these thoughts into the shortest possible sentence. Post the mission statement everywhere you can think of, and repeat it often so that each of your traditions reflects the mission you have established.

One Sample Nursery Mission Statement

Our church nursery provides a physically and emotionally safe environment to facilitate the healthy growth of babies and families into the image and likeness of our Creator. Our staff members serve as ministers. Everything we say and do is centered on the principles of God's Word, which tells us the value of each individual.

Another Sample Nursery Mission Statement

We love and serve babies in the name of Jesus. We are committed to providing a safe and nurturing environment, allowing us to teach babies to love the Lord their God with all their hearts, souls, minds, and strength as they sit, walk, lie down, and get up (Deuteronomy 6). Through that love, we pray that babies will come to know and rely upon God throughout their lives.

Nursery Mission

• What do you want for babies?

• What do you want for parents?

• What do you want for workers and volunteers?

• What do you believe about the relationship between God and babies?

• What do you believe about the relationship between the church and babies?

Appendix C: Play Ideas for Toys

Commercial Nursery Toy: _____

How to Use This Toy

With Holders (three to seven months old):

With Crawlers (seven to twelve months old):

With Walkers (twelve to twenty-four months old):

Maintenance Message

Other Notes

Appendix D: High-Tech Helpers

Use a computer to make many routine nursery tasks simple and visually appealing in a minimal amount of time. Start with these ideas for management and publicity, and let your creativity take it from there.

1. Create your own stationery. Use it for all correspondence. This will help everyone in the church quickly identify your nursery. Create a logo as part of the stationery, and make this a part of all your church communication from announcements to bulletin board headings. You'll be amazed at the impact a frequently used visual image lends!

2. Keep separate computer files of your correspondence to workers, volunteers, and parents. Many times this basic correspondence can be sent again with minimal changes.

3. Create form letters or cards for predictable events such as:
• Welcoming a new baby
• Welcoming a new worker or volunteer
• Baby graduations
• Thanks for extra effort or donations
• Volunteer workers' birthdays and anniversaries
• First tooth
• First steps
• We missed you last Sunday
• Notification of exposure to illness
• Schedule or personnel changes

4. Labels are your best friends. Create a sheet for each baby, and file the labels in each baby's storage space or a flex file. Use them for marking items removed from a diaper bag, babies' art creations, cribs, blankets, or cubbies. Even use them to tag babies themselves by applying the label on the baby's upper back. Adding a scanned photo to these labels is especially helpful if you have new or rotating workers. (Photos of the baby with Mom and Dad on large-size labels help with family identification.) Update all photos at least semiannually.

5. Use the label feature to create mailing labels for class members and workers to simplify correspondence. If you have a goal for frequency of communication (like a once-a-month encouragement note), print the number of labels that corresponds to your goal to help you keep on track.

6. Create photo frames, and post babies' pictures frequently to keep the church family up to date on the latest developments. Create frames for "I have a new tooth!" or "Look who's one now!" Give the pictures and frames to parents as you put up new ones, or save them to present a photo record of the baby's nursery days when the baby moves on to the next class.

7. Create wallpaper borders at babies' eye level (either near the floor or at workers' shoulder height). Cover ink-jet borders with clear plastic adhesive paper. Scanning babies' hands or feet and linking them together can create an especially fun border. Or create a border from their scanned pictures.

8. Try to keep all your artwork in a similar style so that people can identify your look or style. Find cute, kid-friendly graphics in *Group's Best-Ever Children's Ministry Clip-Art* (available from Group Publishing).

Appendix E: Establishing Peaceful Traditions

Routine helps babies feel comfortable. What may seem monotonous to some adults can help babies feel safe, secure, and protected. Whether your volunteer staff rotates weekly or is the same each week, create a predictable and peaceful environment by developing activities and procedures that stay the same each week. We call these "Peaceful Traditions."

Think through a perfect morning. What is it like? What do volunteers say and do for babies? Take a look at the four times below (welcome times, snack-and-bottle times, changing times, and goodbye times), and then write your own traditions on the photocopiable manual page provided (p. 103). Place the traditions in your manual immediately following the cover page so they are easy to refer to.

Welcome—Greet the baby in the same manner each week. Use a puppet, the interactive mural or door activities, or something uniquely yours. Play the same music in the background. Let the babies make both a visual and auditory connection to the nursery. You might even have a signature scent for greeting, such as simmering cinnamon or soft powder air freshener.

Think through your welcoming traditions. Do you want workers to always call the baby by name? To bend down and look a walker in the eye? Specify these traditions that are important to your sense of atmosphere. What do you want volunteers to communicate to parents? How do you want volunteers to greet new parents? Don't leave anything about this critical time to chance. Be intentional about what you do during this time.

Snacks and Bottles—Designate specific areas of the room as snack areas. Keep food and drinks within this area. Think through your snack traditions. Is there a specific time you will serve snacks? Will all babies eat and have bottles on demand? Is there a difference in scheduling for infants and toddlers? Is there a snack-time prayer you'd like babies to become familiar with? Are there manners that are important to you? Make a note of these things so that every worker can follow the same procedures.

Changing Times—How can workers convey that changing time is a pleasant routine? Do you want babies checked for changing needs at specific intervals throughout the morning? We consider changing time as individual attention time. There are several changing play songs in Appendix F that you might use. We also suggest a stash of special changing-time toys to keep babies' hands occupied. Be sure workers are aware of your sanitation policies.

Goodbye Times—Who picks up babies in your nursery? At what time? Do you use songs or little games to make goodbye times more fun? What are some things you want done each week before babies leave? What do you expect parents to do when they are ready to pick up their children? How will you tell each baby goodbye? What will you do to help ensure that parents know what their baby has done this week? We suggest making copies of some of the nursery manual activity pages to send home. Be sure to adapt them for family use by personalizing the "Other Notes" section.

Peaceful Traditions
for Our Nursery

....

Welcome Traditions

Snack-and-Bottle Traditions

Changing-Time Traditions

Goodbye-Time Traditions

Appendix F: Songs for the Nursery

Babies love the sound and rhythmic feel of your singing, whether you can carry a tune or not. In addition to the songs used with specific activities in this book, sing these songs with babies as you rock them, walk them, or play with them to lock the knowledge of God's love deep in their hearts, and to let them know they are precious in your sight too!

Bible-Learning Songs

Use these songs to help a baby learn about God's love and the importance of God's Word.

God Made Me and God Loves Me (to the tune of "She'll Be Coming Round the Mountain")

Oh, God made me and God loves me,
I'm God's child. (Hooray!)
Oh, God made me and God loves me,
I'm God's child. (Hooray!)
Oh, God made me and God loves me,
And that makes me very happy,
Oh, God made me and God loves me,
I'm God's child. (Hooray!)

I Am God's Child (to the tune of "My Bonnie Lies Over the Ocean")

Oh, I am God's child and God loves me,
Oh, I am God's child and God cares,
Oh, I am God's child and God loves me,
And stays with me everywhere.
I love God, I love God, and God loves me, loves me.
I love God, Oh, I love God, and God loves me.

God Loves You (to the tune of "Kum Ba Ya")

You are God's dear child, God loves you.
You are God's dear child, God loves you.
You are God's dear child, God loves you.
Oh, [child's name], God loves you.

The Child God Loves (to the tune of "The Muffin Man")

Oh, have you seen the child God loves,
The child God loves, the child God loves?
Oh, have you seen the child God loves,
Peekaboo! It's you!

Toss a diaper or blanket over the baby's head during this song, and do a tummy tickle on the words "It's you!"

God Gave Us the Bible (to the tune of "The Bear Wcnt Over the Mountain" or "For He's a Jolly Good Fellow")

God gave us the Bible,
God gave us the Bible,
God gave us the Bible,
Because God loves us so.
Because God loves us so,
God wanted us to know,
So God gave us the Bible,
God gave us the Bible,
God gave us the Bible,
Because God loves us so.

Sing this song before you open your Bible story book to share with the babies.

Diaper-Changing Songs

Use these songs to help a baby identify body parts and encourage fun changing times. Wiggle the body parts mentioned as you sing these songs.

The Boo Song (to the tune of "I'm A Little Teapot")

Tiny little hands and tiny little nose,
Tiny little feet and tiny little toes.
God designed your body just the way it's made,
You can trust his plans and never be afraid. (Boo!)

Cover the baby's eyes, and then uncover them on the word "Boo!"

Growing Like God Planned (to the tune of "Twinkle, Twinkle, Little Star")

Big strong arms and small strong hands
You are growing like God planned.
Jesus has a plan for you,
For all you say and all you do.
Big strong arms and small strong hands,
You are growing like God planned.

Have the baby hold on to your index finger as you pull him or her to an upright position and back several times during this song.

The Shakin' Praise Song (to the tune of "Camptown Races")

Put your arms up in the air, praise God, praise God,
Put your arms up in the air, and praise God all day long.
Shake your arms up high, shake your arms down low,
Put your arms up in the air, and shake them very slow.

Mention different body parts during the diaper change. Slip the diaper in when you sing about the baby's legs.

Glad You're You (to the tune of "This Old Man")

Our Lord God, he made one,
God made one belly button,
With a clap-clap, pat-pat,
I'm telling you it's true!
I'm so glad God made you YOU.

Our Lord God, he made two
Little eyes for peekaboo
With a clap-clap, pat-pat,
I'm telling you it's true!
I'm so glad God made you YOU.

Appendix G: Funky Finger Puppets

Finger puppets are lots of fun for babies, whether you choose ones you make or ones you buy in a store.

Easy Puppet: Use a fine-tip pen to draw tiny faces on the baby's fingers.

Sticker Puppet: Attach stickers to a baby's fingers under your constant supervision. These are temporary, but they're fun.

Glove Puppet: Make a puppet glove for yourself. Put a piece of Velcro hook and loop fasteners on each finger of a glove. Create characters out of various sizes of pompoms and wiggly eyes. Attach the corresponding piece of Velcro on each pompom. For a super-simple starter puppet, place the Velcro on the tip top of each gloved finger. Attach five green pompoms, with tiny wiggly eyes glued on the pompom on the pinky finger only. Hold your hand sideways, and wiggle the fingers one at a time to resemble a caterpillar in motion. Use this rhyme:

I'm a little caterpillar.
Watch me crawl around.
God made me very special,
I can move without a sound.

Then encourage the babies to move without making any noise.

Box Puppet: Make puppets in a box. Get a square jewelry box with cotton lining. Cut one, two, or three fingers off a glove, and cut corresponding holes in the cotton lining. Cut matching holes in the bottom of the box with a drill. Put your fingers in the glove fingers and slide on the cotton. Secure the glove fingers to the cotton with glue. Then glue the cotton to the bottom of the box, carefully matching the holes. Decorate the glove fingers to resemble small animals, flowers, or people. Place the lid on the box. When you use the puppet with the children, hold the box in the palm of your hand, carefully inserting your fingers. Knock on the box lid, remove it, and make your fingers stretch as though the puppets are waking up.

Safety Tip: Follow this safety tip. Never leave babies unattended with any removable puppet. Finger puppets can be a choking hazard. Larger hand puppets can cause suffocation.

Appendix H: Ten Ways to Use a Blanket

Blankets are a baby's best friend. Keep plenty around in various sizes, weights, and textures. Try these activities just for fun.

1. Do this activity with an adult partner. Clear a space of all obstacles. Place a baby on his or her back in the center of a heavy blanket. Pick up two corners of the blanket, and have your partner pick up the other two corners. Gently rock the baby in this blanket swing, maintaining eye contact with the baby throughout.

2. Make a tent with a large blanket for crawlers to explore. Make sure the blanket is secured to the top of the table you cover so the babies won't become entangled as they crawl out.

3. Cover a baby with a crib-sized blanket (let the baby tell you whether it's OK to cover his or her face). Have the baby extend his or her arms above his or her head. Hold the baby's hands, and encourage him or her to kick the blanket off.

4. Have an older baby sit on a blanket. A younger baby can lie flat. Pick up two corners of the blanket, and gently pull the baby across the floor. Go *very* slowly until the baby figures out how to maintain his or her balance. Then pick up the pace. Pretend to be a car or a train for extra fun.

5. Let a baby who can walk pull a doll or toy around on a blanket, and challenge him or her to keep the toy on the blanket while walking.

6. Show babies who can walk how to sit on the edge of a blanket and grab the edges, and then use their strong legs to scoot around on the floor.

7. Do parachute activities with a blanket, such as:
• shake the edges to make waves and ripples;
• with two or more babies, raise the blanket up and down;
• with an adult partner, shake a blanket over the babies' heads at various levels, while the babies lie, sit, crawl, or walk underneath.

8. Pile a bunch of soft blankets together so a baby can collapse in the middle of them.

9. Hide a small toy in a pile of blankets, and let older babies dig to find it.

10. Challenge older babies to sit on the blanket while you shift it from side to side.

Appendix I: Ten Ways to Use a Blow-Up Ball

Blow-up balls, often called beach balls, are perfect for nursery use in a variety of ways. Use these ideas to spark your imagination.

1. Partially deflated balls are soft and easier for babies to catch than other balls. Toss a small-sized ball, about three-quarters full of air, and encourage the baby to throw it back to you.

2. To help a baby develop upper body strength, set a baby on top of a partially deflated ball, supporting him or her under the arms. Roll the ball around a small imaginary circle (this will appear to be like a circular rock to the baby) on the floor to stimulate balance.

3. Place a baby on his or her tummy on top of a fully inflated ball. While holding the baby securely, rock the ball side to side and around a small imaginary circle. Older babies enjoy riding the ball all the way into a forward roll. Place one hand on the baby's lower back and one on the baby's head to tuck his or her chin to chest as he or she rolls onto a padded surface.

4. Lay a baby down on his or her back on a large partially deflated ball. Gently push on the sides to bounce the baby gently.

5. Tie string or yarn around the nozzle of a ball (or securely tape the yarn to the ball with masking tape), and suspend it from the ceiling or door frame so that babies can practice batting and catching the ball. Make sure the string holds the ball at baby's-eye level so that it cannot become tangled around any child's neck. Use only under constant adult supervision.

6. Play baby kickball. Hold a baby under the arms, and swing him or her so his or her feet kick the ball. If you have more than one adult, play in teams.

7. Hold two ends of a blanket while an older baby holds the other two ends. Toss a ball on top, and try to keep it from rolling off. For a real challenge, start walking together with the blanket and ball between you.

8. Hold two ends of a blanket while an older baby holds the other two ends. Put a ball in the center, and try to pop up the ball and catch it without pulling the blanket out of your partner's hands.

9. Let babies try to balance a ball on a parking cone (or on a cone made of poster board with a large opening). Note the different challenges of doing this task from a seated or a standing position.

10. Hold a parking cone or a cone constructed from poster board in your hands. Balance the ball on top of it. Turn a hair dryer on the cool setting, and help the baby blow the hair dryer underneath the cone to see what happens. A baby also can help you blow the ball across the floor with the hair dryer as you hold it. Before you do this activity, however, test your hair dryer to ensure that it doesn't heat up *at all* when it's on the cool setting.

Index

A list of activities in this book according to each age group:

With Babies of All Ages:

Activity-Wall Train (Chapter 4: Cozy Corners) 81

Baby Chalkboard (Chapter 4: Cozy Corners) 86

Baby Directory (Chapter 5: Angel Aids) 90

Baby-Safe Bulletin Board (Chapter 4: Cozy Corners) 83

Boo-Boo Bags (Chapter 5: Angel Aids) 94

Fancy, Fruity Finger Paint (Chapter 3: Appealing Art) 48

Funky Finger Puppets (Appendix G) 107

Jelly Bags (Chapter 3: Appealing Art) 58

Learn-About-Me, Fun Flannel Board (Chapter 4: Cozy Corners) 82

A Little Door of My Own (Chapter 4: Cozy Corners) 67

Magical Magnet Board (Chapter 4: Cozy Corners) 85

Mirror, Mirror, Who's That? (Chapter 4: Cozy Corners) 84

My Own Door With Wall Mural (Chapter 4: Cozy Corners) .69

Neat-Scoop Loops (Chapter 3: Appealing Art) 52

Parents' Peekaboo, One-Way Mirror (Chapter 4: Cozy Corners) 65

Play Clay (Chapter 3: Appealing Art) 56

Pocket Belt (Chapter 5: Angel Aids) 92

Pop-Up Puppet (Chapter 1: Together Time) 18

Sandpaper Blocks (Chapter 2: Practical Playthings) 42

Shoulder Apron (Chapter 5: Angel Aids) 88

Soft-Touch Gloves (Chapter 1: Together Time) 24

Songs for the Nursery (Appendix F) 104

Squeeze Art (Chapter 3: Appealing Art) 54

Sticky Collages (Chapter 3: Appealing Art) 50

Ten Ways to Use a Blanket (Appendix H) 108

Ten Ways to Use a Blow-up Ball (Appendix I) 109

Wave Maker (Chapter 2: Practical Playthings) 38

Wiggle Worm (Chapter 2: Practical Playthings) 36

Wonderful, Whimsical Window Art (Chapter 4: Cozy Corners) 62

With Holders (three to seven months old):

Baby Basketball (Chapter 2: Practical Playthings) 34

Baby Bubblers (Chapter 1: Together Time) 14

Baby-Sized Soft Dolls (Chapter 2: Practical Playthings) 32

Cookie-Cutter Puzzles (Chapter 2: Practical Playthings) 40

Indoor Track (Chapter 1: Together Time) 16

Jingle Bands (Chapter 2: Practical Playthings) 28

Lift-and-Peek Books (Chapter 1: Together Time) 20

Look-and-Laugh Books (Chapter 1: Together Time) 10
Puzzle Rug (Chapter 4: Cozy Corners) 77
Reading Rug (Chapter 4: Cozy Corners) 75
Resting Rug (Chapter 4: Cozy Corners) 73
Riding Roller (Chapter 1: Together Time) 22
Road Rug (Chapter 4: Cozy Corners) 79
Tumble Toys (Chapter 2: Practical Playthings) 30
Tunnel Tube (Chapter 1: Together Time) 12
Water-Ballet Bags (Chapter 2: Practical Playthings) 44

With Crawlers (seven to twelve months old):

Baby Basketball (Chapter 2: Practical Playthings) 34
Baby Bubblers (Chapter 1: Together Time) 14
Baby-Sized Soft Dolls (Chapter 2: Practical Playthings) 32
Cookie-Cutter Puzzles (Chapter 2: Practical Playthings) 40
Indoor Track (Chapter 1: Together Time) 16
Jingle Bands (Chapter 2: Practical Playthings) 28
Lift-and-Peek Books (Chapter 1: Together Time) 20
Look-and-Laugh Books (Chapter 1: Together Time) 10
Puzzle Rug (Chapter 4: Cozy Corners) 77
Reading Rug (Chapter 4: Cozy Corners) 75
Resting Rug (Chapter 4: Cozy Corners) 73
Riding Roller (Chapter 1: Together Time) 22
Road Rug (Chapter 4: Cozy Corners) 79
Tumble Toys (Chapter 2: Practical Playthings) 30
Tunnel Tube (Chapter 1: Together Time) 12
Water-Ballet Bags (Chapter 2: Practical Playthings) 44

With Walkers (twelve to twenty-four months old):

Baby Basketball (Chapter 2: Practical Playthings) 34
Baby Bubblers (Chapter 1: Together Time) 14
Baby-Sized Soft Dolls (Chapter 2: Practical Playthings) 32
Cookie-Cutter Puzzles (Chapter 2: Practical Playthings) 40
Indoor Track (Chapter 1: Together Time) 16
Jingle Bands (Chapter 2: Practical Playthings) 28
Lift-and-Peek Books (Chapter 1: Together Time) 20
Look-and-Laugh Books (Chapter 1: Together Time) 10
Puzzle Rug (Chapter 4: Cozy Corners) 77
Reading Rug (Chapter 4: Cozy Corners) 75
Resting Rug (Chapter 4: Cozy Corners) 73
Riding Roller (Chapter 1: Together Time) 22
Road Rug (Chapter 4: Cozy Corners) 79
Tumble Toys (Chapter 2: Practical Playthings) 30
Tunnel Tube (Chapter 1: Together Time) 12
Water-Ballet Bags (Chapter 2: Practical Playthings) 44

Group Publishing, Inc.
Attention: Product Development
P.O. Box 481
Loveland, CO 80539
Fax: (970) 679-4370

Evaluation for *The Warm and Wonderful Church Nursery*

Please help Group Publishing, Inc., continue to provide innovative and useful resources for ministry. Please take a moment to fill out this evaluation and mail or fax it to us. Thanks!

● ● ●

1. As a whole, this book has been (circle one):

not very helpful   very helpful

1   2   3   4   5   6   7   8   9   10

2. The best things about this book:

3. Ways this book could be improved:

4. Things I will change because of this book:

5. Other books I'd like to see Group publish in the future:

6. Would you be interested in field-testing future Group products and giving us your feedback? If so, please fill in the information below:

Name _____

Street Address _____

City _____ State _____ ZIP _____

Phone Number _____ Date _____